THE RESURRECTION

THE RESURRECTION

A DIALOGUE

by

G. W. H. Lampe

and

D. M. MacKinnon

Edited by WILLIAM PURCELL

THE WESTMINSTER PRESS

Philadelphia

LIBRARY OF CONGRESS CATALOG CARD NO. 67–12284

Published by The Westminster Press ®
Philadelphia, Pennsylvania

PRINTED IN THE UNITED STATES OF AMERICA

Acknowledgements are made to the B.B.C. for permission to use such material incorporated in this book as originally appeared in their programme 'Meeting Point'.

CONTENTS

I

HOW THIS DIALOGUE BEGAN

HOW THE DIALOGUE AROSE

I

HOW THIS DIALOGUE BEGAN

UNIVERSITY teachers find themselves invited from time to time to emerge from their lecture rooms and place some of the results of their thinking before much wider audiences. In the case of the members of a Faculty of Divinity this often takes the form of an invitation to occupy a pulpit or to deliver an address in a broadcasting studio; sometimes to use both these media by broadcasting a sermon preached in church.

At Easter, 1965, I attempted to present the 'good news' of Christ's Resurrection to a mass audience through a televised sermon delivered at a service of Holy Communion in a great parish church. In the evening of the same day this sermon was the subject of a discussion in the B.B.C.'s programme, 'Meeting Point', in which I was questioned by some members of the morning congregation under the chairmanship of Canon W. E. Purcell, editor of this Dialogue, and at that time the Religious Broadcasting Organizer for the Midland Region of the B.B.C. This discussion evoked a very large correspondence which did not entirely cease until nearly the end of the year.

At a late stage in this correspondence my colleague in the Cambridge Faculty of Divinity, Professor D. M. MacKinnon, wrote me a valuable letter critically questioning me about the views which I had expressed. Some years previously, he, too, had broadcast on the subject of the Resurrection. This had taken the form of a meditation, broadcast in the Third Programme, and hence, of course, intended for a quite different audience from that to which my sermon had been addressed. In the course of conversations between us, arising out of his letter to me and my reply to it, it occurred to us that it might be useful to publish a dialogue about the foundation stone of our common faith. We have, therefore, taken our respective broadcasts as our theme, and have commented on them in relation to each other. We have not attempted to imitate the style of direct conversation, but our respective contributions have been discussed between ourselves, and we have taken account of views which we have expressed in talking to one another.

Those who undertake an honest search for truth in a matter of deep Christian concern must expect to arouse strong feelings. Our object, however, is not to engage in controversy. Our views differ in certain highly important respects, and in our comments we have naturally concentrated our attention on these points of difference, and tried to explain our reasons for them. Our statements, however, are by no means antithetical, and we are not trying simply to score points for and against them. We hope, rather, that they may be complementary, and that by setting out our views side by side in a popular rather than a technically theological fashion we may jointly contribute somewhat more towards the understanding of the Easter gospel than we could achieve separately.

G. W. H. LAMPE

AN EASTER SERMON

G. W. H. Lampe

Preached in St Martin's, Birmingham Parish Church, at a televised Communion Service on Easter Day, April 18th, 1965, this sermon formed the basis of the discussion which was to follow that evening in the programme Meeting Point *on B.B.C. 1. All those who were to discuss it then were present among the large congregation. Professor Lampe began his sermon with a text from* 1 Corinthians 15. 17.

AN EASTER SERMON

G. W. H. Lampe

'IF CHRIST was not raised, then our gospel is null and void, and so is your faith. . . . But the truth is, Christ was raised to life.' When Paul wrote these words he was face to face with a crisis of belief: the crisis of belief in which we also stand. One thing there was that he held on to: a fixed conviction that a man who had been executed, who was dead and buried, was alive now, a living person: that, so far from that man's death being the end of him, he was Paul's own Lord and Master, the one whom he must follow, trust in, and obey if his life was to have any meaning. How could Paul believe anything so fantastic? Because he was absolutely convinced that Jesus, who had been sentenced to death at the instigation of Paul's own friends for reasons of which he thoroughly approved, had encountered him personally with shattering effect. For that experience had turned his whole life and all its values upside down. It had made him devote the rest of his life, at the cost of immense risk and suffering, to the one task of spreading the good news: that God had said 'Yes' to Jesus; that his way of life had been vindicated; that what he did and said had been true after all; that love, understanding, forgiveness, self-sacrifice are the real things that matter in the end.

And Paul believed that many others before him had been encountered by the living Jesus. He can give names; most of those people were still alive when he was writing. For them, too, Jesus had come alive. He had gripped them.

Their lives had been turned upside down, too. They hadn't dreamed it up for themselves. It had come to them out of the blue, when they were least expecting it. And they had become Jesus Christ's men: Christians.

Paul himself was actually on his way to round up some Christians and take them to jail when a flood of light dawned on him and he heard a voice saying, 'I am Jesus whom you are persecuting'. Not a voice you could record on a tape. No-one else heard it.[1] The only words Paul could find to describe what happened are, 'He was seen by me also'. He doesn't mean 'seen' as you see me now with your two eyes. He means that a revelation came to him: in the way that one might see God. And there are moments in life when one *does* see God. For Paul and all those others before him Jesus became a living reality, and, for ever after, that was the one thing that really mattered for them.

That is the Easter story. Forget, if you will, the picture, beloved of the old artists, of a body, holding a flag of triumph, stepping out of a grave. That suggests a corpse come back to life on this physical plane. If that were what the idea of Christ's resurrection means, then it were better forgotten. Such a Christ is dead. He remains buried. The real Christ is not a revived corpse. He lives in the fullness of God's life. He is the life, the truth, the way, for us. He lives for us and in us. For the experience of Easter didn't stop with Peter, Paul and the rest. The living Christ may encounter us too, very often in our relationships with other people. And, for what it may be worth, I know that he has gripped me: in so far as his love compels me to try to follow him, inspires me, encourages me, and forgives me for what I am. How this can be is mystery. But I am sure, as Paul was, that if all this is a delusion then one might as well be dead. If it can't be true in the real world, then the real world is no place to live in. 'At its heart the world is not

[1] See page 36.

mad but sane. That is the bare minimum of faith for man. Without it we cannot live, but only take a long time to die.'

But is the world mad or sane? On one dark day it seemed mad indeed: that day we call Good Friday. Here was one whose whole life was grounded in trust in God: in the certainty that God is good; that he can be called 'Father'— and not only by Jesus himself but also by all those who learn from him to say 'Our Father'. Here was one who was ready to accept people as they were, with all their unlovableness, understand them, and make them his friends; one who met hatred with love and forgiveness; one who showed up the selfishness of complacent people, condemned it and made them begin to hate it too; one who so moved people that they changed their whole outlook and became his followers. His love and forgiveness extended to everyone except those who were wilfully blind to it. It included even those who murdered him. And he believed that in all this he was speaking and acting with the authority of God; that this was the real truth about the way things are.

But it wasn't. That Friday was the end. God, if there was a God, had turned away. The life of Jesus had proved to be a catastrophic mockery: one of those great ironical jokes that history sometimes plays with the best of men. Jesus died with the cry 'My God, my God, why hast thou forsaken me?'—the only time that Jesus did not call God 'Father'. God had let him down. The real world belonged to Caiaphas and his power-politics, to the religious institution with its privilege and its jealousy, to Pilate with his anxiety about his career, to the mob who yelled for Barabbas because Barabbas was all that they could understand. Faith in a God like the God of Jesus didn't work out in the end: and Jesus was dead. 'There came a darkness over the whole land': for the light of the world was quenched.

Until Easter morning. And then suddenly and against all possible expectation some of his friends, those who had all deserted him, had that same experience that later came to Paul. He encountered them. The light shone for them in a new way, to lead them on: as it shines through all history in those who follow him. Jesus now was not just a remembered figure of the past, but their living Lord. God who had seemed, if he cared at all, or if he existed at all, to have said so decisive a 'No' that Jesus was dead and buried, had said 'Yes' to Jesus: to his faith, his love, his forgiveness.

For Easter speaks about God. It is not a story of a return of a dead person to this life. It has nothing in common with what a surgeon might do if he got a heart moving again after it had stopped. It has nothing to do, either, with the idea that there is some part of our being that is inherently immortal: some entity that we might call a soul. No. As far as our human nature is concerned, when you're dead you're dead; and so was Jesus. Still less does Easter say that death is unreal. It's brute fact, all right. The Easter experience tells us that God *is*; that faith in God won't let us down; that Jesus' way of life, his trust in a God of love, was justified; that a life of faith in God and so of love and acceptance of other people, was vindicated for him and can be vindicated for us too. God has said the last word about it; and that word is 'Yes'. God's affirmation of Jesus is stronger than what we foolishly call the real world; it is stronger than death itself. God *is* the God whom Jesus taught us to call 'Our Father'. He *is* the God of love: love which will not let us go, even through death. Here, if we follow Jesus, the living Lord, lies our hope of reaching that perfect relationship with God which, because God is unchanging, we call eternal life. Not this kind of existence going on and on, but life transformed by faith and love so as to become life of a different quality.

The Easter experience, that Jesus is the living Lord who claims us as his followers, cannot be demonstrated to be true like a scientific proposition. The Lord encounters us in a personal relationship, and personal relationship is not susceptible of objective proof. There was no objective demonstration at Easter that Jesus had won the victory. He was never seen by Caiaphas or Pilate or the Jerusalem mob. It would be childish to think that there could be some dramatic confrontation between the risen Lord and his enemies. For God says 'Yes' to the man who is willing to trust him. He cannot speak to those whose hatred and complacency makes faith and trust impossible. Such people had mocked Jesus, saying, 'Let the king of Israel now come down from the cross and we will believe him'. He never did come down for them, not even by a resurrection. For them he was still dead.

There is no proof of that kind. Only the assurance of experience. The experience of those whose eyes were opened to know Jesus as their Lord at Easter; the experience of those who wrote the New Testament; for those books were written *because* Jesus was known to be the living Lord, and otherwise no Christian would have put pen to paper; indeed, there would *be* no Christians. And the experience of ourselves, which we are going to renew today as we meet at the Lord's Table, to take bread and wine in remembrance of him and find that he comes alive again for us and in us. This is assurance enough.

And if this is true, then the world is not mad. It is sane: because it is God's world. Our pessimistic assumptions that the real world is a world of selfish rat races, that real people must be hard-faced, are profoundly unrealistic. In the last resort things work out in the way of the God whom Jesus called 'Father'.

This doesn't mean that the world of inhumanity is all an illusion. It's there all right. And so it must be at the cost of carrying his cross that Christ's men have to follow in the way of love and acceptance and forgiveness. Easter does not guarantee an easy comfortable time all round. On the contrary, the unquenched light of the world shines most brightly in the long line of the martyrs, from Peter and Paul at Rome in the year 65 or thereabouts to James Reeb in Selma, Alabama, in the year 1965. The good news of Easter is that the last word doesn't lie with Emperor Nero or Governor Wallace any more than it did with Pilate and Caiaphas. Nor does it lie with our own worse selves. Our worse selves may raise a clamour about nigger neighbours; our worse selves may be occupied more quietly in just keeping up with the Joneses until the only competition left is who can afford the costlier funeral; in either case if that were the last word how right Paul was: our gospel is indeed null and void. 'But the truth is, Christ was raised to life.' The last word is with those who, like Peter and Paul, asked for prayers for Nero; with those demonstrators who prayed that they might love Wallace; with all of us who want to follow Jesus. For the first and last word is God's Word, the Word made flesh, Jesus Christ, our risen Lord.

THE TELEVISION DISCUSSION

In the Meeting Point *programme, televised on the evening of Easter Day, six people—four men and two women—assembled to question Professor Lampe on the sermon they had heard him preach that same morning. The six included two university lecturers: Dr Brewer, then a member of the English Department at Birmingham, and Dr Gowenlock, a member of the Department of Chemistry in the same university. There was also a teacher of theology from the Methodist Ministerial Training College in Handsworth, Dr William Strawson, together with a member of the staff of St Martin's Parish Church, the Rev. Christopher Mayfield. The two ladies were Mrs. Jill Bell and Mrs. Monkhouse, both of Birmingham. After a brief introduction from the Chairman, Canon Purcell, and the showing of some traditional pictures of the Resurrection, the programme proper opened with a recorded extract from Professor Lampe's sermon.*

3

THE TELEVISION DISCUSSION

LAMPE: 'If Christ was not raised, then our gospel is null and void, and so is your faith. . . . But the truth is, Christ was raised to life.' When Paul wrote those words he was face to face with a crisis of belief: the crisis of belief in which we also stand. One thing there was that he held on to: a fixed conviction that a man who had been executed, who was dead and buried, was alive now, a living person: that so far from that man's death being the end of him, he was Paul's own Lord and Master, the one whom he must follow, trust in and obey if life for him was to have any meaning. How could Paul believe anything so fantastic? Because he was absolutely convinced that Jesus, who had been sentenced to death at the instigation of Paul's own friends for reasons of which he thoroughly approved, had encountered him personally with shattering effect. For that experience had turned his whole life and all its values upside down. It had made him devote the rest of his life, at the cost of immense risk and suffering, to the one task of spreading the good news: that God had said 'Yes' to Jesus; thus his way of life had been vindicated; that what he did and said had been true after all; that love, understanding, forgiveness, self-sacrifice are the real things that matter in the end. And Paul believed that many others before him had been encountered by the living Jesus. He can give names: most of those people were still alive when he was writing. For them, too, Jesus had come alive.

He had gripped them. Their lives had been turned upside down, too. They hadn't dreamed it up for themselves. It had come to them out of the blue, when they were least expecting it. And they had become Jesus Christ's own: Christians. Paul himself was actually on his way to round up some Christians and take them to jail when a flood of light dawned on him and he heard a voice saying, 'I am Jesus whom you are persecuting'. Not a voice you could have recorded on a tape. No one else heard it.[1] The only words Paul could find afterwards to describe what had happened were, 'He was seen by me also'. He doesn't mean 'seen' as you can see me now with your two eyes. He means that a revelation came to him: in the way one might see God. And there are moments in life when one *does* see God.

That is the Easter story. Forget, if you will, the picture, beloved of the old artists, of a body, holding a flag of triumph, stepping out of a grave. That suggests a corpse come to life again on this physical plane. If that were what the idea of Christ's resurrection means, then it were better forgotten. Such a Christ is dead. He remains buried. The real Christ is not a revived corpse. He lives in the fullness of God's life. He is the life, the truth and the way for us.

PURCELL: Amen. So much for that. Now to our questions. Mrs. Bell.

BELL: Professor Lampe, you said this morning, referring to the sort of pictures we have just seen, that they suggest 'a corpse come back to life on the physical plane', and that 'If that were all that the idea of Christ's resurrection means, then it were better forgotten'. Why is it better forgotten? Is one not able to believe that Christ was resurrected in a physical form and still be an intelligent

[1] See p. 36.

Christian? After all, it is what the Church has believed for two thousand years, isn't it?

LAMPE: I shouldn't want to say at all that it isn't possible to be an intelligent Christian and take the story of the empty tomb as a literal historical fact. After all, a great many highly intelligent Christians do so. I do not, myself. I regard the story of the empty tomb as myth rather than literal history, and profoundly significant as myth. But what I was getting at in my sermon was not exactly that point. It was rather that, whether you take the empty tomb story literally or as a mythical description of what we mean by the Resurrection (namely that the living presence of the crucified Christ is present with us now), the idea is better forgotten, or rather is better not entertained at all, that the Resurrection is parallel to the raising of Lazarus from the grave in the Fourth Gospel. That was somebody who had died coming back to this life. He was not glorified. He didn't enter into a new and higher mode of life. He did not become the source of new life for us. That was the sort of event which might make us marvel. We might say about it, 'Oh wonderful' or 'Oh, how extraordinary', but it would not necessarily communicate God to us at all; and Christ's Resurrection does communicate God to us.

BELL: But Mary Magdalene and the other Mary clasped the feet of the risen Jesus. This is recorded in St Matthew. If he wasn't in physical form, how could this be?

LAMPE: Your question raises the whole problem of the nature and value of the historical evidence for what happened at Easter. This is a vast subject, and perhaps other questions that may be asked will bring us back to it again. For the moment I will only say that the Resurrection narratives contain material of very different and sometimes apparently contradictory kinds, and of unequal historical value. I think it is clear that the earliest and most reliable tradition, as you find it in St Paul, tells us of appearances of the risen Lord: of an experience of vision, an objective, compelling and convincing revelation that Jesus was not dead, buried and forgotten, but was here and now the living Lord. I think the earliest tradition is in that form and not in terms of a physical resurrection.

BREWER: But isn't it the case that if we say that the story of a physical resurrection of Christ is a legend, the legend is in direct opposition to what you are supposing to be the actual truth, that is, that Christ's body rotted? The legend would therefore be a lie?

LAMPE: No. I don't think that is the right way to think of it. I think that the question of historicity is finely balanced, and one can't afford to be dogmatic about it. Certainly not negatively dogmatic, and I think not positively dogmatic either. But I think there is good evidence that the tradition about the Resurrection was gradually built up in the course of the growth of the New Testament. As I see it, it starts with the experience which St Paul describes by saying that the risen Jesus was seen by so-and-so and so-and-so, and by himself: that is, in the encounter on the Damascus road. Then, naturally, people began to think about the question of what gave rise to that experience: about what the mechanism of it was, as one might say. This would produce the stories of the empty tomb. But no deliberate falsification is implied.

BREWER: Yes. But as the story is told, presumably only one of only two things could have happened. Either the body of Christ was physically raised or it physically rotted. There is a dilemma here. The story, or myth, says that it was raised, and that is in direct opposition to what you contend is the implication of the most reliable tradition.

LAMPE: Oh, of course, there is direct opposition. It's perfectly clear that either the body somehow emerged, was removed or disappeared from the tomb, or it remained there. But what you find in the New Testament, I think, is, first, people who were convinced through mysterious experiences that Jesus was, in fact, actually with them as their Lord and Master. Then the tradition shows that the question began to be explored of how this might have come about; and, particularly in a Jewish environment where there was a strong belief in a future bodily resurrection, the natural explanation would have been that Jesus' physical body emerged to life out of the grave.

GOWENLOCK: You said this morning that when Paul refers to his vision of the risen Christ 'he doesn't mean "see" as you see me now with your two eyes; he means that a revelation came to him'. And of the disciples you said, 'On Easter morning Jesus encountered them'. Now in what ways do revelation and encounter differ from self-induced hallucination and delusion?

LAMPE: I don't know whether you would agree with me here, but I don't think there is any kind of built-in quality about a revelation or an experience of encounter which in itself distinguishes this from a self-induced hallucination. You cannot differentiate between them simply by reference to the strength or vividness of the experience itself; for an hallucination might be extremely powerful. I don't think there is any built-in criterion here. I think you can only apply the test, 'By their fruits you shall know them'. What persuades me that the Easter stories of the Resurrection appearances are true and that something objective happened to those people, which was not mere hallucination, is first of all the context in which they seem, according to the records, to have taken place. They seem to have come straight out of the blue and not in a situation where anything of the kind might have been expected to occur. Secondly, there is the consonance of that experience with the subsequent experience of Christian people.

GOWENLOCK: You are implying, then, that there is no contact here with objective reality, as some people might define objective reality. I mean, something outside oneself—or is it outside oneself?

LAMPE: I think this is extraordinarily difficult. We are on very delicate philosophical ground when we begin to try to draw a hard and fast dividing line between subjective and objective. I don't know how one could do it.

GOWENLOCK: But you would say, then, that at any rate the relationship is personal.

LAMPE: Yes.

GOWENLOCK: And that there is some sense of continuity of relationship involved in all the Resurrection appearances.

LAMPE: Yes, indeed I do. It seems clear that there was a very deeply convincing and moving experience: so moving and convincing that it changed all these people's lives and has gone on changing the lives of people who try to understand it. And this was undoubtedly an experience of relationship: a personal relationship with Jesus which was renewed and recreated.

BREWER: This is the sort of question that really underlies a good deal of the problem: the question of the nature of the evidence for the Resurrection. It is clear that St John's Gospel is different from the other three, though the other three have minor differences. St John's Gospel is much more concrete even than the others about the physical reality of the risen Christ. But from what you said you appear to deny the physical reality of the risen Christ. I wonder what you think really happened.

LAMPE: I think the last part of your question is almost impossible to answer: 'what really happened?' That's because here, you see, we come back to Dr Gowenlock's point about the subjective and objective aspects of the event. The people from whom the tradition originated were absolutely convinced that there was an encounter, which they hadn't dreamed up for themselves, between the objective presence of Christ, 'outside' themselves, and their own selves. That happened. I think you have got exceedingly strong historical evidence for that, evidence which is very early indeed because the tradition had come to Paul himself from the first Christians. He actually mentions names, and appeals to the witness of people still alive who had had that experience. Above all, what impresses me is the experience of Paul himself, which we have got at first hand. He couldn't say much about it. I don't think he could describe what happened; but he knew that somehow or other he had met the Lord.

BREWER: Is St John's Gospel any help in this, do you think? In the way he talks about the grave-clothes. You remember it says the head cloth was in one place . . .

LAMPE: Yes. I was just going to question your remark about the Fourth Gospel being much more concrete than the others about the physical reality of the risen Christ. I don't think that this Gospel simply stresses the physical aspect of the Resurrection, as such. I think there's a steady build-up of the tradition of the empty tomb through the Synoptic Gospels. But when you get to the Fourth Gospel I am always impressed by the way in which, although it seems to be literalistic, yet when it makes us look at the arrangement of the grave clothes, to which you referred, it doesn't suggest at all that there is a body which has *emerged*: in such a way, I mean, that if Pontius Pilate had happened to be walking past the garden at the right time he would have seen it happen. I don't think the Fourth Gospel thinks like that. In its description of the arrangement of the grave clothes it suggests that the physical body has simply *gone*. Then, I think, this Gospel goes on to lead the reader beyond the point where one is concerned with the physical body of Christ; and in the story of Thomas it shows that faith is not to be established by sight; that you have got to look beyond any objective truth of the kind which might be established by visible, tangible, corporeal manifestations: to look beyond that to something different. And I think the something different is the kind of experience Paul speaks of.

MAYFIELD: If we have got to look beyond the objective proof to some experience, many people would ask, 'Is there any objective proof in the first place?' This is the stumbling block. Is there any objective proof or isn't there? And if we can't have an objective proof, are we not in the position of having to say that the Resurrection is null and void and the life of Jesus Christ was a hopeless failure?

LAMPE: No. I'm sure we aren't.

MONKHOUSE: Could we consider it from another angle, not looking so much at St Paul's experience, which might have been hallucination, but looking at it from the point of view of the Church, which is the only objective verifiable result of the Resurrection? While maintaining a reverent agnosticism about what happened physically, can we not look on the Resurrection as the birth of the Church and the continuation of its life through the ages?

LAMPE: Yes, certainly. I very largely agree with you, Mrs Monkhouse. I think the great objective proof, if you can talk in those terms (and I'm not sure if you really can)—the nearest, at any rate, that you can get to objective proof of the Resurrection—is the birth of the Christian Church, this community of people who live by faith in the living Lord, and the continuity of that community down the ages in that same faith. I think that's the tangible thing that you've got. But I wouldn't go all the way with you, because the existence of the Church itself depends, doesn't it? on the testimony of certain people like Paul and like the others before him (Peter and the rest) whom he points to as original witnesses on the basis of whose testimony the Church itself started. So I think there is a little difference between us here. For I don't think that the truth is simply that the Church is the Resurrection. I think the Church represents a kind of gathering up of an experience of Christ as the living Lord, and that this begins with certain people who did in fact have this direct and immediate experience of a quite shattering kind.

STRAWSON: This morning, Professor Lampe, you said, 'As far as human nature is concerned, when you're dead, you're dead'. Now what I want to know is, What other sort of nature is there beside human nature, and how does this connect with the age-old Christian belief that there is a personal destiny, a continuity of some kind between this life and the life hereafter? If as far as human nature is concerned we are dead, then what nature survives, if any?

LAMPE: Well, I will tell you what I was trying to say this morning. I don't know how effectively it was said, but what I was driving at was this. I believe that when we come face to face with the prospect of death there is nothing in ourselves and nothing built into ourselves which we can trust in. When we come face to face with death I don't think we can say to ourselves, as it were: 'Well, all right. This body is going to dissolve, but I am confident that somewhere in me there is a sort of built-in "me", a soul or what have you which is inherently immortal. So I can put my trust in that and I know that come what may I am going to survive in some way.' I don't believe that. I believe that when we come face to face with death we are face to face with annihilation, so far as we are concerned. There is nothing in us to give us hope or confidence. Our confidence and hope seem to me to rest entirely and solely in God. That is what I think the Easter message is about. It is about God's personal relationship with us, his love and care for us, surviving death. I believe that this relationship that we have with God, which is all his doing and is due entirely to his initiative (for it is God taking hold of us and making us his own), is stronger than death because God is eternal and unchanging. I believe that this is what is demonstrated at Easter.

GOWENLOCK: You are saying, then, that the relationship which Jesus had with his disciples survived the physical death of Jesus, and you are now saying, too, that our relationship of faith and trust in God survives, or can survive our death through what he does.

LAMPE: That's what I believe, yes. And I believe it, I think it is true to say, against all ordinary human probability. I think it is a matter of sheer faith in God, and I find that faith justified for me by the experience of those first Christians and by the continuing experience of the Church that relationship with God through Jesus survived his death.

STRAWSON: But is this relationship only for people in the Church, or is everyone in some sense in a relationship with God?

LAMPE: Everyone is in some sense in a relationship with God. They must be, mustn't they, if one gives the kind of meaning to the word 'God' that I think all of us would want to give?

STRAWSON: So we are all going to heaven?

LAMPE: I don't know about that at all. Who can say? I shouldn't want to put it in quite those terms, anyway— though I should find it very difficult to believe in God if I didn't believe also that his care extends to all his creatures.

BREWER: But isn't this completely diluting the Church and dissolving the Church into all the rest of humanity?

LAMPE: No. I think there are two questions here which are getting rather confused. One is: 'Is everybody in some sort of relationship with God?' That is what Dr Strawson asked me. Yes, of course; because otherwise God would surely not be God. The other is: 'Is there a more limited number of people who are in a particular relationship to God through their acceptance of Jesus Christ as Lord and through their recognition that, because of that relationship, they are sons of God?' Yes, there is.

MONKHOUSE: I wonder, Professor Lampe, if you could tell us anything about the relevance of the Resurrection to the present day. Humanists and Christians both try to do the best they can for people in the world, and these good works are surely good in themselves. Does the Resurrection help us at all to understand the difference?

LAMPE: I am sure that humanists and Christians do the same good works, works which are of equal value as such. I also believe that the Easter message of the Resurrection of Jesus Christ provides a new context or dimension in which the Christian can set this doing of good works. It puts our relationship to other people on a different footing by placing it in the perspective of relationship to God. This perspective extends beyond the limit to which the humanist can follow, because faith in the living Christ transcends death. But, of course, if you ask me precisely *how* this relationship to God survives death, that is, *how* we shall be recreated in a continuing relationship with God on the other side of death, one simply cannot answer.

4

EASTER

A STATEMENT

G. W. H. Lampe

Among the questions put to Professor Lampe in the
Meeting Point *discussion as reproduced in the
previous chapter, one was : 'Is one not able to believe
that Christ was resurrected in a physical form and
still be an intelligent Christian? After all,' the
questioner added, 'it is what the Church has believed
for two thousand years, isn't it?'*

*The beginning of Canon Lampe's reply was as
follows : 'I shouldn't want to say at all that it isn't
possible to be an intelligent Christian and take the
story of the empty tomb as a literal historical fact.
After all, a great many highly intelligent Christians
do. I do not, myself. I regard the story of the
empty tomb as a myth rather than literal history,
and profoundly significant as a myth. . . .'*

*Both question and reply gave rise to a great deal of
correspondence, much of it, as regards the latter,
highly critical. In the light of that reaction, and as
an integral part of the dialogue in which he has
subsequently been engaged with Professor Mac-
Kinnon, Professor Lampe prepared a statement
which forms the basis of the following chapter.*

4

EASTER

A STATEMENT

G. W. H. Lampe

NEITHER in my sermon nor in the subsequent broadcast discussion of it was the fundamental question about Easter directly raised. This is the question whether what happened at the first Easter was an objective event in the external world or whether it was simply a change of mind, radical and dramatic but not necessarily sudden, on the part of the disciples. Was the Resurrection an event in the life of Jesus, so that we can say that God actually raised him from the dead? Or was it only an event in the lives of the disciples—a change in their outlook as they came to realize through further reflection upon their dead and buried Teacher, that his influence still lived on, that his teaching had been true, that his life must be their example and his character a pattern for themselves to follow, that although he was dead he must still be revered in their memory as their Lord whose spirit could still be recreated in themselves in so far as they dedicated themselves to the aim of following in his footsteps? When we say that Jesus was raised from the dead are we speaking literally or metaphorically? Do we mean that he was raised in the minds of his disciples: that as they remembered him and began to put a new and higher value on his words and deeds he seemed to be still so real to them and so uniquely important that they found that they could think of him as though he were still with them? Or are we making a factual assertion, not only about the mental processes of the disciples but about Jesus himself? Are we saying that, however mysterious and inexplicable the event may be, Jesus was actually made alive, in a new and glorious mode of existence, although he had really died and been buried?

Professor MacKinnon and I agree in the belief that the Resurrection was an event in the external world: that Jesus was actually raised from the dead. In holding this belief we differ from some recent writers on the subject of Easter. They maintain that Jesus 'rose' in so far as his followers came to understand his true significance. My sermon, on the other hand, asserted in the strongest possible terms that the Resurrection was a fact, attested by a series of events which those who experienced them described, in so far as they could be described in human language, by saying that Jesus 'appeared to them' or 'was seen by them' alive. Like Professor MacKinnon in his Easter meditation, I based my sermon on the assumption that there was an objective Easter event, and that it was this event which produced the dramatic change in the outlook of the disciples; that to speak of 'Easter' is not a way of describing the disciples' growing conviction that Jesus had been right after all; but that it was only because something real and objective and totally unexpected had actually happened at Easter that the disciples became changed men.

I did not discuss the other possibility. My reason for this was because I find it incredible. All the indications in the Gospels suggest that at the time of the arrest of Jesus the disciples lost all hope and faith in Jesus. They all forsook him and fled, except Peter, and he very soon denied all knowledge of him. Unless something extraordinary happened to convince them that against all their expectations God had reversed his apparent verdict on Jesus, I cannot imagine that they would later on have taken immense risks to assert in public that a man who had been condemned and hanged was no less than God's Messiah. It proved difficult enough to persuade the world that this was so, even when it was proclaimed by men who believed that God had raised him from the dead. Without that belief I think it inconceivable that the first disciples could have even entertained the idea themselves. The attitude of the Qumran community to their revered 'Righteous Teacher' offers no adequate parallel, and I cannot think that, apart from the Resurrection, a fundamental change of mind on the disciples' part about the true significance of the crucified Jesus is historically probable or that it is sufficient to account for the origin of the Christian Church. The 'Pentecostal' enthu-siasm of the disciples arose, not from reflection about the value of a dead man's deeds and words, but from the conviction that that man was alive as Lord and Messiah and that they could testify from their experience of actual encounter with him that God had glorified him.

Having deliberately passed over in silence the possibility of a purely subjective interpretation of the 'Resurrection' and committed myself as strongly as I could to the belief that at Easter certain things actually happened which persuaded a number of people that God had truly raised Jesus from the dead, I expected a vigorous rejoinder from those who take the view that I had ignored. I was surprised to receive no 'come-back' of this kind. Among the great number of correspondents who wrote to me after this broadcast there were many who attacked my presentation of the Easter message; but these were not, as I had expected, sceptics or unorthodox Christians, but the orthodox themselves. Some of these had totally misunderstood what I had said. They accused me of reducing the Easter event to a mere change of outlook on the part of the disciples, or, in the manner of Bultmann, to a decision on our part, at this present time, to accept as our Lord the Christ who encoun-ters us in the Easter preaching of the Church, to which the whole question of an event alleged to have happened two thousand years ago is irrelevant. Many others, who did grasp my meaning, were dismayed because, while I asserted the objective reality of God's act at Easter, I did not take the stories of the empty tomb as the basis of my interpretation of that act of God, but, on the contrary, suggested that these stories may be unhelpful to our understanding of the Easter message. The controversy which followed this broadcast was therefore not about the fact of the Resurrection (except where my meaning had been misunderstood), but about its nature: about what we may believe to have actually happened at Easter. The question is whether the good news of Easter, 'The Lord is risen indeed' (Lk. 24. 33), may or may not be true without what is implied in the invitation of the angel to the women at the tomb, 'Come, see the place where he was laid' (Mt. 28. 6).

Some may think that it is profitless to discuss 'what we may believe to have actually happened'. The Resurrection, they may say, is not an event on the same plane as other events. It is a unique act of God. It lies outside the purview of the historian and it is not open to investigation by the methods of ordinary historical inquiry. There are those who would add that it is an event which belongs to the realm of 'salvation history', and that 'salvation history', that is, the process of the working out of God's plan for man's salvation, is not accessible to the historian. Its events belong to the sphere, not of history in the ordinary sense, but of the supra-historical; they cannot be objects of historical research because they are discernible only by faith.

Now it is perfectly true that it is only to the eye of faith that certain historical events may reveal the operation of God's saving purposes. Faith alone can discern a mighty act of God in the Exodus from Egypt. The historian as such cannot tell us whether or not the Exodus belongs to 'salvation history'. But he can tell us whether or not it is probable that the Exodus from Egypt ever happened; and if he were to tell us that in all likelihood the whole story is unhistorical then it would cease to be for us a revelatory event, since it would have ceased to be an event. The story could still be told, but as a myth. It would be a fictitious story expressing certain timeless truths or beliefs in the form of a concrete and particular narrative. Such truths or beliefs might perhaps be that patient endurance gets rewarded in the long run, that one should never despair even in impossible circumstances, that tyrants tend to come to a bad end, and so on. But the myth cannot offer any assurance that the beliefs are well-founded; it is only a pictorial way of expressing them.

So, too, with the Resurrection. It is true that the historian cannot pronounce upon the significance which faith discerns in what happened at Easter. That Jesus was raised by God and exalted as the Lord of glory is not a statement which the historian as such has any grounds either for affirming or denying. It lies outside his province. It is an assertion that is possible only to faith. But faith makes this assertion on the basis of certain things which are recorded as having actually happened at Easter. The claims which Christian faith makes are an interpretation which it puts upon these happenings; and the historian has every right to investigate the records of these happenings and to pronounce upon the probability or otherwise that they did in fact occur. If the result of the inquiry were to be that it is exceedingly improbable that any part of the record is true, then the Easter story becomes a myth and not a part of history (and hence not a part of 'salvation history'). And to maintain that, if an event belongs to 'salvation history' or is 'supra-historical', it lies outside the province of the historian not merely to judge whether the interpretation which faith puts upon it is justified or not (which is true), but to investigate whether it ever happened or, if it did, what kind of thing it was that happened, is tantamount in practice to saying that it is mythical.

Some might be content, as I said before, to relegate the Resurrection to the category of myth. This would not deprive the Easter story of all value. It would then be an attempt to convey in a vivid pictorial form the truth, or the belief, that self-sacrificing love is so supremely valuable that in comparison with it even death is of small significance; that although the enemies of Jesus won their victory over him, yet in retrospect his life has become a more potent influence than theirs, for his memory has survived as an inspiration and example for all men. But this is not what either the first disciples or all later Christians have meant by the Resurrection. Paul's life was not turned upside down because he reflected on the value of Jesus' life and decided that goodness, even in defeat, is a more potent force than triumphant evil. He was convinced, against all his previous beliefs, that the same Jesus who had been crucified had encountered him objectively as the living Lord who now claimed his obedience.

A myth of 'resurrection' might certainly express the hope that goodness prevails over wickedness in the long run. It might even encourage men, in the face of despair and death, to hope against hope: perhaps to echo Job's cry, 'Though he slay me, yet will I trust in him'. But it could offer no assurance either that there is a God or, if there is, that he is a God who cares and who will not let us down. It can afford no real answer to the cry, 'My God, my God, why hast thou forsaken me?'

We have to be concerned, then, both with the question, 'What happened at Easter to awaken the Christian faith that God raised Jesus from the dead?', and with the question, 'What does the belief that Jesus was raised from the dead mean to us?'

My sermon was intended to show something of the meaning of the Resurrection for us. In it I said that I am convinced that the Resurrection, as something that really happened, is the one thing that assures us that in the last resort the world is not mad but sane. It is the evidence that there really is a God, that he is the God of love, and that we can call him 'Our Father'. Because God raised Jesus from the dead, after his life had seemed to end in tragedy, we can be sure that faith in God will not let us down. If, on the other hand, nothing actually happened at Easter and if, therefore, the Christian faith which rests upon the Resurrection is a delusion, then we might as well be dead. For it is only if we believe that death was not the end of Jesus, the one man whose trust in God was complete and perfect, that we can accept Paul's brave advice: 'Stand firm and immovable, and work for the Lord always, work without limit, since you know that in the Lord your labour cannot be lost'.

What, then, did happen? The friends of Jesus, and afterwards Paul himself who had been, until that moment, an active enemy and persecutor of the first Christians, found that Jesus, who had died and been buried, encountered them as their living Lord and claimed them for his service in the world. The evidence that this happened to them is good. Paul gives us first-hand testimony that Jesus appeared to him. He also tells us of many people before him to whom the same experience had come, beginning with Peter and the other original disciples of Jesus and including five hundred people most of whom were still alive when Paul was writing, which was some twenty-five years or rather less, after the Crucifixion (1 Cor. 15, Gal. 1. 16). We also have a fuller account of Paul's encounter with the risen Lord in Acts 9, repeated in Acts 22 and 26. This may represent an early tradition of that event, handed down in the Christian community, perhaps at Jerusalem, rather than Paul's own account of the matter; but it is consistent with what Paul says himself in his own letters. There are also accounts of appearances of the risen Jesus in the Easter stories in the Gospels of Matthew, Luke and John.

It is not possible to say precisely what the nature of these experiences was. That is not surprising. Their effect was shattering, and especially in the case of Paul, the enemy of the Christian movement, they had the effect of turning upside down the whole outlook of the people concerned and reversing the course of their lives in the most drastic and complete way. An experience of that kind is scarcely describable. Paul himself speaks of it, in his own case and in that of the others before him, in terms of sight: 'He appeared' or 'was seen'. The word used here generally denotes a vision of God or of 'God's angel'. We cannot say whether Jesus was actually seen with the bodily eyes in some kind of physical form (so as to have been capable in theory of being photographed). I think, however, that this is highly unlikely. According to Acts, what Paul experienced when, as he tells us, the Lord appeared to him (or was seen by him) was a blinding light and the hearing of a voice speaking to him. Acts 22 and 26 suggest that his companions may also have seen the light (the three accounts in Acts are not consistent on the point of whether the whole experience was private to Paul or not),[1] but they saw no one. More important, these appearances were not primarily *proofs* demonstrating objectively to the world in general that Jesus was alive. They were the way in which the risen Lord called men to his service; hence to be a witness of the Resurrection was to be a missionary. God reveals his activity in claims to faith and obedience, not by demonstrative proofs outside the sphere of his call to particular men whom

[1] Acts 9. 7 and 22. 9 are contradictory about the hearing of a voice. For the sake of brevity my sermon assumed the story as related in 22. 9 and confirmed by implication in 26. 14. See page 8.

he chooses, though it remains true that his revelation in these ways may become evidence to us (although not proof) that God is, and that he is a gracious God.

Of course, the evidence of Paul, at first hand, and of many others which we know about primarily through Paul (his letter to the Corinthians is considerably older and closer to the events than the earliest of the written Gospels), is open to the objection that we have no guarantee that the appearances were not hallucinations. Some people are disturbed by the idea that Christian faith may rest only upon the testimony of certain individuals to have experienced a vision of Jesus after his death. It seems to them that this is an insecure foundation on which to build the whole structure of Christian belief and the way of life which follows from it; especially since such experiences may not be unique, for there are possible parallels, not only in the visions of the saints but in many alleged psychic phenomena. Can these appearances rank (as Acts 1. 3 claims) as 'ample evidence that he was alive?' Is there no assurance of a more objective and less disputable kind?

The objection has considerable force. There is no guarantee in the records that the Easter appearances were not a series of hallucinations, including a mass hallucination of the five hundred people. I do not think we need be dismayed by this. It is consonant with what Christians believe about the manner in which God reveals himself. He makes his activity known to faith, and faith is not compatible with unmistakable proofs. It was precisely this desire for some infallible external guarantee which Jesus resisted when he was tempted to test his experience of receiving a divine call at the time of his baptism. The temptation was to throw himself off the Temple roof and challenge God to preserve him unhurt. It was this same desire which he refused to satisfy for other people when they asked him to give them a sign from heaven. There can be no objective proof that Paul and the others were not self-deceived.

On the other hand, it is important to observe that they were not expecting to meet Jesus as their Lord. In Paul's case this is obvious; he was persecuting the Christians because he thought that Jesus had been a false prophet or bogus messiah. It is hard to think that his experience on the road to Damascus was a piece of unconscious self-deception or wish-fulfilment. And it seems clear from what took place after the arrest of Jesus that Peter and the other disciples had no hope that this would happen. Jesus probably foresaw his own death; but I think it is almost certain that the passages in the Gospels which speak of this, and which in some instances go on to say that he prophesied his resurrection, have been written up and embroidered in the light of what actually happened at Easter. Only in the obviously late and legendary story of the guard at the tomb (Mt. 27. 63) is there any clear indication that a resurrection was expected, and this story is evidently related to controversies between Christians and Jews in Matthew's own day, many years after the event and at a time when the subject of dispute was the empty tomb. It runs counter to the general evidence about the disciples' state of mind at the time of Jesus' death, all of which suggests that the experience of encounter with the living Lord was something which, as I said in my sermon, they had not dreamed up for themselves, but which 'came to them out of the blue when they were least expecting it'. This tells to some extent against it being hallucinatory.

It is also proper to ask whether the effect of that encounter on their own lives, and through them on their contemporary world, is more consonant with it being genuine than with being an hallucination. I think that the answer is yes. It is also legitimate to adduce the continuing experience of Christian believers down to the present day. This is not the same as that of Paul or the others to whom he refers. It does not take a form which could be described by saying 'He appeared to me.' The Easter appearances lasted for a brief period only and Paul was aware that the appearance to him was the last of the series. After it the presence of the Lord was no longer mediated in visual or auditory encounter. Yet Christians continue to be encountered by his living presence in other modes, and the reality of their experience is more easily understandable, to say the least, if the appearances at Easter were a real encounter with an objective presence.

I do not think that the subjectivity of 'vision' and 'hearing' renders the Easter appearances inadequate as an assurance that God truly raised Jesus and that he won the decisive triumph over death. If the appearances to the apostles were private manifestations, in the sense that a casual bystander would have seen nothing: if, that is to say, they were in the nature of visions rather than of bodily seeing, this does not imply that these men were not confronted with the Lord's presence as an external reality. To maintain the contrary would be to pass a very sweeping and damaging judgement on a great body of religious experience. It would be hard to think that because, in all probability, no other worshipper in the Temple saw anything remarkable when Isaiah 'saw the Lord, high and lifted up' (Is. 6. 1 ff.), therefore the prophet dreamed up that experience and the Lord's presence never impinged upon him in objective reality. It does mean, however, that, as this example from the Old Testament indicates, the Easter appearances were not dissimilar in kind from other phenomena in the history of religious experience. I see no reason why this should not be so. God's revelation in Christ is final and complete; but the Gospel events are not the only point at which God has revealed himself to men, and since there is continuity in the substance of revelation there is no need to be surprised if there is also continuity in the modes in which it is communicated.

In the discussion which followed the sermon, I was questioned about this passage in it. 'Forget, if you will, the picture, beloved of the old artists, of a body, holding a flag of triumph, stepping out of a grave. That suggests a corpse come back to life on this physical plane. If that were all that Christ's Resurrection means, then it were better forgotten. . . . The real Christ is not a revived corpse. He lives in the fullness of God's life. He is the life, the truth, the way for us.'

The question was: 'Is one not able to believe that Christ was resurrected in a physical form, and still be an intelligent Christian? After all, it is what the Church has believed for two thousand years, isn't it?' To this I replied: 'I should not want to say at all that it isn't possible to be an intelligent Christian and take the story of the empty tomb as a literal historical fact. After all, a great many highly intelligent Christians do so. I do not, myself. I regard the story of the empty tomb as myth rather than literal history, and profoundly significant as myth. But what I was getting at in my sermon was not exactly that point. It was rather that whether you take the story literally or as a mythical description of what we mean by the Resurrection (namely, that the living presence of the crucified Christ is present with us now), the idea is better forgotten, or rather is better not entertained at all, that the Resurrection is parallel to the raising of Lazarus from the grave in the Fourth Gospel. That was somebody who had died coming back to life. He was not glorified; he did not enter into a new and higher mode of life; he did not become the source of new life for us. That was the sort of event which might make us marvel. We might say about it, "Oh, wonderful", or, "Oh, how extraordinary", but it would not necessarily communicate God to us at all; and Christ's Resurrection does communicate God to us.'

Here are the reasons why I do not take the story of the empty tomb as factual history, but as an attempt to express the implications of the Easter appearances in terms of a story or picture (i.e. as a myth). Some of these reasons are historical. The earliest account of the Easter events is made up, first, of the first-hand testimony of Paul, who had no doubt that his encounter on the Damascus road was to be classed among the Easter appearances (in adding, 'though this birth of mine was monstrous' (1 Cor. 15. 8) he is alluding to a difference in his own condition as compared with the first disciples, not to any difference in the nature of the appearance). Secondly, the account comprises Paul's recitation of a tradition of similar appearances to others before him (1 Cor. 15. 3 ff.). This was part of what he calls 'the facts which had been imparted to me'. By this he means that it had been passed on to him long before he wrote this letter to Corinth, probably, indeed, soon after his conversion. It therefore goes back to the earliest days; it is extremely important evidence, and we are on relatively sure historical ground here. It is true that the tradition contains the assertion that the Resurrection, like Christ's death, took place 'according to the scriptures'. This need not, however, mean that the story had already either been invented or modified in order to square with Old Testament prophecies. The mention of 'the third day' (1 Cor. 15. 4) suggests that the scriptures which the tradition had in mind were Hosea 6. 2 and possibly Jonah 1. 17 (conceivably also 2 Kings 20. 5, by a far-fetched interpretation). Now none of these texts corresponds very readily to the tradition of the Easter event. It is unlikely that they would, as it were, catch the eye of a Christian reader searching the Old Testament for prophecies about Christ, and induce him to think up a story to show that an important prophecy had been fulfilled. It looks much more as though these texts caught the eye, and were regarded as prophetic, only because it was already known, on the testimony of witnesses of the Resurrection appearances, that Jesus was actually encountered as the living Lord on the third day after his death. The prophecies are probably adduced to support this testimony, rather than vice-versa. This being so, it is an important fact that this very early account of Easter makes no mention of the tomb being found empty. Neither does what Paul tells us about the appearance to himself suggest that he thought of this in terms of a bodily manifestation (and the account of it in Acts indicates clearly that Luke believed it was not). These earliest testimonies thus stand in contrast to the Easter stories in the Gospels, where the empty tomb is a central fact and the appearances of Christ are thought of, in the light of this, as being in some cases bodily: involving touch as well as sight, and including eating in the presence of the disciples. They indicate that the Easter message that Christ has been raised from the dead was originally based historically on a series of appearances rather than on a discovery that his tomb was empty. The reference in the ancient tradition to the fact that Jesus had been buried (1 Cor. 15. 4) does not necessarily imply a belief in a bodily resurrection, and, since there is no mention here of the empty tomb, it probably does not; rather, it indicates the reality and finality of Jesus' death (he had been actually dead and buried), and just possibly hints that in his burial the prophecy of Isaiah 53. 9 had been fulfilled. The whole of this passage of Isaiah was of great importance to Christians as pointing to the fact that the paradoxical death of the Messiah was part of God's plan, and later on this particular verse may have influenced the development of the detailed story of Nicodemus and the burial of Jesus.

If Paul and the tradition which he cites lay no emphasis on the empty tomb the question arises whether Paul nevertheless may have known of it. Many New Testament

scholars hold that he did.[1] Certainly it would be quite un-
safe in the ordinary way, to infer that he did not from the
fact that he does not actually allude to it. But in this case
I think that the argument from silence has unusual force.
For the situation in which Paul wrote 1 Corinthians 15 was
that some of the Corinthians were denying that there is a
resurrection of the dead (1 Cor. 15. 12). In answer to them
Paul marshals every possible argument, and in particular, he
adduces the known fact that Jesus was raised from the dead
as the foundation for belief in the future resurrection of
Christian people. If Jesus' Resurrection is denied, he says,
the bottom drops out of the Christian gospel. And the
evidence that he was raised consists in the appearances to
himself and to others. Had he known that the tomb was
found empty it seems inconceivable that he should not have
adduced this here as a telling piece of objective evidence.

In the same chapter he maintains that Christ's Resurrection is the first-fruits of our own. It is the assurance that
Christ's people will also be raised. The argument rests on
the belief that his Resurrection was not different in kind
from what they may look forward to through trusting in
him. It is therefore important to see what he says in answer
to the question, 'How are the dead raised?' (1 Cor. 15. 35 ff.).
Since Pharisaic Judaism held a strong belief in the resurrection of this mortal body, and Paul belonged to this tradition (see Acts 23. 6), it might be expected that Paul would
affirm that belief. At one time, indeed, he does seem to have
thought of the future resurrection in this way. In 1 Thessa-
lonians 4. 14 (probably his earliest letter) he says: 'We
believe that Jesus died and rose again; and so it will be for
those who died as Christians; God will bring them to life
with Jesus. . . . We who are left alive until the Lord comes

---

[1] They include my colleague, Professor C. F. D. Moule. See his footnote
(p. 122) in his important article, 'St Paul and Dualism' (*New Testament Studies*,
12, 2, January, 1966).

shall not forestall those who have died; because . . . the Lord himself will descend from heaven; first the Christian dead will rise, then we who are left alive shall join them, caught up in clouds to meet the Lord in the air. Thus we shall always be with the Lord.'

This is the traditional imagery of Jewish apocalyptic. The picture suggests a bodily resurrection of the dead and a transference of the living directly from this world to another. But Paul is not content simply to reproduce this traditional picture. He gropes after some way of expressing a more original conception of resurrection; and one reason why he does this may probably be because his belief in future life came to be founded much more upon his own Easter experience, and that of the others whom he mentions, than upon Pharisaic and apocalyptic tradition. So in 1 Corinthians, having asked how the dead are raised, he attempts to answer the question by saying, on the one hand, that there is some kind of real, though indefinable, continuity between our present bodily mode of existence and the life beyond death, and, on the other, that there is discontinuity also. He cannot grasp the nature of this continuity, for it is a mystery; but it seems to him that there is an analogy in the relation of the grain that is sown to the corn that grows up. His point is that what comes up in the farmer's field is not the same thing which was sown. The seed, indeed, suffers dissolution. The corn has a different kind of 'body' from the seed. Yet, although corn and seed are different, there is an organic connection between the two.

So it is with the dead. The body which is put in the grave is not raised as a physical body. 'Flesh and blood can never possess the kingdom of God, and the perishable cannot possess immortality' (1 Cor. 15. 50). What is 'sown' is 'an animal body'; what will be raised is a 'spiritual body'. Paul is quite clear that the body of flesh and blood no more emerges from the grave than the seed itself comes up out of the ground. And yet the new form of existence, the 'spiritual body' (that is, a body made for life on a different plane of existence, life with the risen Christ), is not entirely unrelated to the body of flesh and blood. 'It is raised', says Paul, 'as a spiritual body'. If we ask what he means by 'it', he cannot precisely tell us; but he is evidently groping after the idea that 'we', that is our personalities, will be re-made by God for a different mode of existence from that of the flesh-and-blood body, and yet that in some way we shall retain our identity and be the same personalities as those which now live in the mode of physical beings. This will be so, even though the physical structure is not raised as such (compare 1 Cor. 6. 13).

Elsewhere Paul lays less emphasis on the element of continuity, or rather, perhaps, he expresses it somewhat differently, finding the continuity between this life and the next in our 'selves' rather than in any organic link between the physical body and the spiritual body. In 2 Corinthians 5. 1 ff. he says: 'We know that if the earthly frame that houses us today should be demolished, we possess a building which God has provided—a house not made by human hands, eternal, and in heaven. In this present body we do indeed groan; we yearn to have our heavenly habitation put on over this one—in the hope that, being thus clothed, we shall not find ourselves naked.' He thinks of the present body as 'demolished' in death. And yet he wants to say that it will be our whole selves which will enter into new life. It is not merely some one part of our make-up which will be brought to life again: naked, as it were, and without any mode of self-identification and self-expression corresponding, in a spiritual existence, to the physical body in our earthly existence. In Philippians 1. 22–24, again, Paul contrasts 'departing' (from this life) 'and being with Christ' with 'staying on in the body'.

In the light of this profound and difficult thought about the resurrection of believers, and bearing in mind that he believed Christ to have been the pioneer or 'first-fruits' of those who will be raised like him, I find it difficult to think that Paul could possibly have believed that Jesus rose from the grave as, or in, a physical body. 'Flesh and blood can never possess the kingdom of God.' But if the body of the risen Christ could be handled, and if he truly ate food, then this is untrue; flesh and blood manifestly did possess the kingdom of God. I think we can be reasonably sure that those Resurrection stories which speak of a fully corporeal presence of Jesus after his death could not have been known to Paul. It is not so impossibly difficult to think that he could have believed that the physical body of Jesus had been transformed in the grave into a spiritual body, and that it was no longer there at Easter because it had been changed into another substance which did not exist spatially. Perhaps he did believe this; but his language about the grain and the corn, and especially the way in which he speaks of the dissolution of our bodily frame, makes me think it improbable that he could have thought that the coming into being of the spiritual body involved the disappearance of the flesh-and-blood 'framework': that the corpse itself must disappear. It thus seems to me probable that the earliest stratum of the Easter tradition did not make the gospel depend upon an empty tomb. The Easter stories in the four Gospels, on the other hand, come nearer to doing this. These stories are somewhat different in character from the main body of the Gospels, especially in the case of the first three (the Synoptic Gospels). They have, like the Infancy narratives, the characteristics of myth. Angels, visible in human form, appear as characters in the narrative and address the chief actors; an angel descends from heaven, rolls away the stone which sealed the rock tomb and sits upon it. The stories of the appearances of Christ combine traditions about a

'spiritual body' such as Paul speaks about (the Lord appears
suddenly within a room) with others which tell of a tangible
body, capable of being touched or grasped and of the physical
process of eating. More obviously than in other parts of
the Synoptic Gospels there is much material which is
evidently a casting back, in the form of a narrative about
Jesus, of the thought and experience of the Church in later
years, and of its controversies with opponents. The narratives in the various Gospels are remarkably inconsistent
with each other (e.g. Luke insists that all the Easter events
took place in or just outside Jerusalem; Matthew that it
was in Galilee that Christ was seen by the disciples). They
are all clearly independent of the very early tradition
recorded by Paul, and in some respects are very difficult
to reconcile with it.

It may be as well to give a brief summary of the stories in
the first three Gospels. In *Mark* three women come to the
tomb on the morning of the first day of the week to anoint
the body. They see that the huge stone has been rolled
away. Inside the tomb they find an angel (a young man in a
white robe, a regular way of describing a supernatural
being). They are stricken with amazement, as in most
stories of angelic appearances. The young man calms them,
tells them that Jesus is not there because he has risen, and
gives them a message for the disciples and Peter, that Jesus
is going on before them to Galilee and they will see him
there. But the women run away in terror, and say nothing
to anyone. Here Mark's original Gospel ends. A late and
spurious conclusion has been added. Whether Mark intended
to finish his book at this point, or whether an authentic
ending was somehow lost before it had ever been copied
is a matter of dispute. I think that the former view is much
more probable.

The point of this story is contained in the angel's words
to the women. These words explain that the tomb is empty,

not because the body has been taken somewhere else, but because Jesus has risen, presumably in corporeal form. They also point to a Resurrection appearance in Galilee. The fact that the women do not pass the message on may suggest that the evangelist, or his source, knew that the story of the tomb and the angel was not part of the original Easter proclamation and had only developed at a relatively late stage in the tradition.

Mark is generally held to be the earliest Gospel, written some thirty-five to forty years after the events. The order in which Luke and Matthew follow Mark is uncertain. Probably they were both written between fifty and sixty years after the events that they record, and I am inclined to think that the order is Luke–Matthew. All the evangelists, of course, used written sources (though in Mark's case this cannot be demonstrated for certain) and oral traditions; and Mark's Gospel was a source used, in the opinion of most scholars, by both Luke and Matthew.

In *Luke* Mark's brief story is evidently used, but it is drastically altered. Three women as before (but the name of one is different) go to the tomb. The stone has been rolled away. The body is found not to be there. Then two men in dazzling garments (i.e. angels) suddenly appear at their side. The women are terrified, but the two men tell them, not that the disciples are to go to Galilee, but that they themselves are to remember that while Jesus was in Galilee he had prophesied that he would be crucified and would rise again. The men also ask them why they are looking among the dead for one who is alive. The women do report this to the apostles, but their story is taken to be nonsense, and is not believed. Some manuscripts here add that Peter, however, did then go to the tomb, looked in and saw the grave-clothes, and went home amazed; but this is not certainly a part of Luke's own story, and it may have been introduced from the Fourth Gospel at a later stage.

Thus far Luke has followed Mark in broad outline, but the account of the empty tomb has been built up in rather more detail, the saying of the angel(s) to the women has been completely recast in line with Luke's view that all the Easter events happened at Jerusalem, and not in Galilee, and the women are said to have informed the disciples. Luke's version still suggests that the empty tomb was not part of the original tradition; for although in Luke the women do not 'say nothing about it to anyone' (as in Mark) their report is disbelieved.

Luke then adds further information. Two disciples encounter Jesus on the way to Emmaus, but do not recognize him. He converses with them and reinterprets the Old Testament for them, showing that in every part of it the suffering and glorification of the Messiah was prophesied. Finally, at supper with them, he takes bread, blesses, breaks and gives it to them. Then they recognize him and at once he vanishes from their sight. This story also includes a reference to some disciples having gone to the tomb and found it as the women had reported, but having not seen Jesus. This may refer to the visit of Peter mentioned earlier, if this is authentically Lucan.

When the two disciples return, the eleven apostles and others tell them that the Lord has meanwhile appeared to Peter. This episode is, no doubt, the same as that appearance to Peter which comes first in Paul's list in 1 Corinthians, and is thus part of the very early tradition. It is very awkwardly integrated by Luke with the Emmaus story, and looks as though it comes from a tradition which was originally quite independent of it, and probably also of the rest of the Synoptic Resurrection narratives.

While this is being discussed, Jesus suddenly appears among the disciples in the room at Jerusalem. They think he is a ghost; but he invites them to touch him and see that he has flesh and bones (contrast Paul's language about flesh and blood). He then takes a piece of fish, and eats it before their eyes. Then, as on the way to Emmaus, he expounds the Old Testament as a body of scripture referring to himself, assures them that it was written in these scriptures that the Messiah should suffer death and rise again and that repentance and forgiveness should be proclaimed to all nations in his name. He commissions them as witnesses of all this, promises that they will receive the gift of the Spirit, and bids them remain in Jerusalem until then, since their mission is to start from Jerusalem (compare Isaiah 2. 3, Micah 4. 2). He leads them out to Bethany, blesses them, and parts from them (and, according to most manuscripts, ascends to heaven).

In Acts, Luke's second volume, a period of forty days elapses before the Ascension, during which Jesus discourses with the disciples and commissions them as witnesses. He then ascends bodily, while two men in white (i.e. angels) interpret this to the disciples.

These stories that are peculiar to Luke seem clearly (with the exception of the appearance to Peter) to embody in the form of myth the experience of the post-Easter Church. They show that the Old Testament can, and must, be read as a Christian book, prophetic of Jesus; that the paradox that the Messiah should suffer death can be understood in the light of the scriptures; and that the risen Lord's presence, even if it is not recognized at other times, is to be discerned when he encounters his people in the breaking of bread (the Church's Eucharist). They also reflect controversies about the Easter appearances. It was evidently being objected that the appearances may have been hallucinations, or that what the disciples saw was merely a ghost. In answer to this it was being asserted that the presence of the risen Lord was corporeal, tangible and possessed of flesh and bones: this despite the obvious inconsistency with the Pauline tradition and with elements incorporated in Luke's own narrative, namely, the sudden appearance within a room and the seemingly simultaneous appearance to the two disciples at Emmaus and to Peter at Jerusalem.

In *Matthew* Mark's narrative is followed more closely but with a number of elaborations. It is introduced by a story which obviously reflects later controversies with the Jews. Christians were claiming that the tomb was found empty; Jews were replying that the disciples must have stolen the body away. A Christian apologetic argument had then been developed, which Matthew incorporates: the Jewish authorities had heard that the disciples were expecting a resurrection; they therefore got Pilate to post a guard at the tomb. After the Resurrection had happened, the guard reported to the authorities, who bribed them to say that while they were asleep the disciples stole the body. This legend, which is very much in the manner of the later apocryphal gospels, is interwoven with the Marcan narrative. It is obviously a reflection of the controversies of Matthew's day, and has no historical value.

In Matthew's main narrative two women, not three, go to the tomb. Instead of the stone being already rolled away, there is a violent earthquake, an angel descends, rolls back the stone, and sits on it. 'His face shone like lightning, his garments were white as snow.' He tells the women that Jesus is not there, but has been raised; and he gives them the message for the disciples which Mark had recorded. The women run to tell the disciples this, but on the way Jesus meets them and gives them greeting. They clasp his feet and fall before him. He then repeats the message given by the angel: the disciples will see him in Galilee. Matthew then adds a story which tells how they did see Jesus on a mountain in Galilee, and worshipped him, though some doubted. Jesus assures them that all authority has been committed to him in heaven and earth (that is, he is the Lord). He commissions them to go and make all nations his disciples, to teach them his commandments and baptize them; for he will be with them always.

Thus, like Luke, Matthew embodies in a Resurrection story the conviction of the Church that the raising of Jesus from the dead, as the Lord of all men, meant that its task must be to witness to him and to preach him as Lord to all the nations, although, as Acts shows, the realization that the gospel was meant for all nations, and not only for the Jews, came gradually as a result of further revelation, and could not have been an instruction given at Easter.

The analysis of the Synoptic narratives of Easter suggests that, while they are full of profound theological reflection about the Christian experience of the risen Lord (especially the Emmaus story), they are of much less historical value than the tradition recorded by Paul. They suggest that the story of the empty tomb may not have been part of the first proclamation of the Easter message, and that the story itself has undergone a process of building up (at least if Mark's brief account was all that that evangelist himself offered). They suggest that, apart from a parenthetical allusion in the Emmaus narrative, and a doubtfully authentic mention of Peter going to the tomb, the disciples themselves were not concerned about the tomb at all. Either the women did not tell them, or they did tell them but they disbelieved the report, or (in Matthew) the women told them, but the important part of their message was that they should go to Galilee and the disciples therefore went on there without taking any action about the tomb. Except in those Matthaean additions which are generally agreed to be legendary, the tomb is not the main focus of interest even in these Gospels, and attention is concentrated rather on the appearances of Jesus.

This indicates a reply to those who argue that if the tomb was not empty the enemies of Christ had only to show his body in the grave to refute the whole basis of Christianity.

This may not be so. Even assuming that Jesus' grave was known, which is by no means certain, it seems very possible that neither party was interested in it, or regarded the truth of Easter as dependent on it, until long after the event: until the period of the controversies reflected in Matthew, which would not arise until the empty tomb had become important in Christian thought about the Resurrection. It should be observed that the Christians, on their part, showed no disposition to point to the grave of Jesus, or exhibit it, when they preached his Resurrection, any more than their opponents referred to it.

The Synoptic narratives, taken at their face value, show considerable confusion about the nature of the appearances. Sometimes the risen Presence is bodily: indeed, fleshly. At other times this is not so. The risen Christ appears suddenly in the midst at Jerusalem, or vanishes at Emmaus. If they were of the latter kind, consistently with the Pauline record, then they were not appearances of what is meant by the term 'body'. In that case, if they were in the nature of visions (which does not imply unreality) or manifestations of a spiritual body, the old artists' picture of a material body emerging from the tomb is altogether incongruous. We may, however, grant that the evangelists do not speak of an 'emergence'. Matthew's angel rolls away the stone, not to allow the body to emerge, but to show that it is no longer there. This suggests a transformation into a spiritual or dematerialized 'body'; but, as I have suggested before, there seems no reason to suppose that a re-creation of the 'self' in a different dimension of existence should involve the abolition of the material flesh and blood. The empty tomb would still be unnecessary to the Easter story. Such an interpretation, too, would seem inconsistent both with those narratives which speak of a material body of flesh and bones being seen by the disciples and also with the insistence of later Christian preaching (e.g. in Luke's speeches in Acts) that the flesh of

Jesus was raised without having seen corruption (in fulfilment of Psalm 16. 10). To suppose that the body of Jesus
was 'dematerialized' in the grave, but from time to time
'rematerialized' seems altogether pointless. More important, this would do away with that correspondence of the
Lord's Resurrection with our own which was fundamental
to Paul's argument about future life and is vitally important
for our own belief about it.

Bodily resurrection, therefore, to which the empty tomb
would be appropriate, and a raising to a new and non-
material dimension of existence, to which it would not,
seem to be confusedly woven together in the Synoptic
traditions when these are taken as factual records. One must
add that if the Resurrection were to be conceived of in a
material way the question will arise, 'What happened to
the risen body of flesh and bones in the end?' Luke may
have had no difficulty in answering this: it went up, spatially,
to heaven. For us that reply is impossible. Indeed, as early
as Origen in the third century it was being pointed out that
we must not think of the Ascension as a movement in space;
and in fact Luke seems to have translated into mythical
form, i.e. a pictorial narrative, the universal belief of the
early Church that Jesus has ascended to the throne of God,
not in a physical manner but in the sense that he has been
exalted to Lordship over all the world.

In fact, however, as I have indicated, I do not think that
the Synoptic traditions should be taken for the most part as
factual history, but rather as reflections, cast in narrative
form, of the theological thinking of the early Church about
the Easter appearances and of various current controversies
about them.

The Fourth Gospel offers, in my view, a most profound and
moving meditation on the traditions used by the Synoptists,
in the light of the experience of Christian believers who truly
encountered the risen Lord in the worship and witness of

the Church. Its narratives contain many echoes of the stories in Mark and some of those which occur in Luke, and the evangelist has modified and added to the earlier traditions (his Gospel is generally agreed to be the latest of the four) in such a way as to make them the vehicle for a great body of deep religious truth.

The story begins with Mary Magdalene, alone, going to the tomb while it was still dark (an impressive piece of symbolism). She finds the stone removed, and runs to tell Peter and the 'beloved disciple' that the Lord's body has been taken away. These two then run to the grave; the 'beloved disciple' looks in and sees the grave-clothes lying there. Peter goes inside and sees the wrappings arranged in order (there is an intentional contrast here with the raising of Lazarus, still helplessly bound in grave-clothes). The other disciple then enters, sees, and believes. The author adds that they did not yet realize from the scriptural prophecies that Jesus must be raised; if they had discerned the truth from scripture, it may be implied, the sight of the tomb would have been unnecessary, as it is for Christians now. They then go home; but Mary stays at the tomb weeping for the body which she thinks has been taken away. She looks in and sees two angels where the body had lain. They ask her why she is weeping, and she explains her sorrow that the body is no longer there; indeed, Mary identifies the body with 'my Lord'. Then she turns and sees Jesus; she does not recognize him, but takes him to be the gardener who may have removed the body; but when Jesus calls her by name she realizes that he is 'my Master'. Jesus says, 'Do not cling to me, for I have not yet ascended to the Father'; and she is told to tell the disciples, not that he is going to Galilee, but that he is ascending 'to my Father and your Father'. She gives the message to them, saying, 'I have seen the Lord'.

On the same evening Jesus appears in the midst of the disciples, though they are in a room with locked doors, and commissions them to proclaim the gospel which brings forgiveness or condemnation (according to the way in which it is received), breathing upon them the Holy Spirit. Thomas, who was absent, is told about this, but refuses to be convinced of the living presence of the Lord unless he can see and touch the wounds in the body of Christ's flesh. Next week Jesus appears once more, again behind locked doors. Thomas is invited to do precisely what he had said would alone give him assurance, but, without touching Jesus, he confesses him as 'my Lord and my God'. In answer, Jesus declares that faith is not to be dependent upon sight: 'Happy are those who never saw me and yet have found faith' (like the believers of the evangelist's own day).

To try to interpret the meaning of this narrative in detail would require a long chapter to itself. It is not possible to attempt it here. One element in it, however, stands out. This evangelist has taken the stories of the empty tomb and of a material Presence of the risen Lord, has accepted them, but at the same time has indicated, subtly but emphatically, that the essential truths of Easter are not to be found in them. Faith does not need to be confirmed by sight. The scriptural witness of the prophecies should be enough as a basis for faith; Mary did not find the Lord through her quest for his body, but only through answering his personal call to her; she must not cling to his bodily presence, for his life is now on another plane, with the Father who is the Father of all those who follow Jesus because he is *his* Father who has raised him from the dead; Thomas is offered sight and touch, as a gracious concession to his lack of faith; but he does not believe because of this, but because the risen Lord addresses him; and the happiness of those who have faith without sight is greater.

So the Fourth Gospel, while offering us, on the surface, a materialistic presentation of the Resurrection, leads us through it to a deeper interpretation related to the Church's continuous experience of the risen Lord.

The last chapter of this Gospel may perhaps be by another hand. It records an appearance in Galilee, reminiscent of the tradition in Matthew and the implications of Mark; but it is connected with a miraculous catch of fish which, or a story parallel to which, is placed by Luke at the time of the call of the first disciples at the beginning of Jesus' ministry. As in Luke, it symbolizes the scope and success of the apostles' mission to the world, to catch men. It includes a meal by the lake-side where the Christian experience of meeting the Lord at the Eucharist is reflected back into the Easter story; and it leads up to the rehabilitation and commissioning of Peter as the leader of the mission, a foreshadowing of his death, which had happened, of course, long before this Gospel was written, and a discussion of the destiny of the 'beloved disciple', possibly John. All this is, I think, a reading back of the circumstances of the later apostolic mission into the time immediately after that Resurrection which was the reason for the mission, the basis of it, and the power which inspired it.

It remains to ask why, if the empty tomb is not an original or essential part of the Easter message, it came to take so prominent a place in the story. The answer is that this was very natural. Once Christians began to reflect on the original proclamation that God raised Jesus and that he was seen alive by many witnesses, they would naturally picture the event of his raising in terms of an empty grave. Particularly would this be true of men who were accustomed to the beliefs of Pharisaic Judaism about future life; though the tendency would not be entirely confined to them. But the natural inclination to picture it in this way would be greatly stimulated by reflection on the scriptures. When Christians searched the Old Testament for texts bearing on the Resurrection they would be struck by Psalm 16. 10: 'Thou wilt not abandon my soul to Hades, nor let thy loyal servant suffer corruption'. This prophecy was a powerful weapon in the armoury of Christian apologetic. It is cited in Acts 2. 27 and Acts 13. 35.[1] It would immediately suggest that the raising of Jesus ought to be conceived in terms of a physical resurrection of the body. From that point the story would inevitably come to be built up, as we can see it growing in the Gospels.

These are the historical reasons why I told my questioner that I did not myself accept the story of the empty tomb. I must, however, admit at once that they are not conclusive, for at every point other students of the New Testament might disagree with my exegesis. The interpretation of these documents leaves room for much difference of opinion. When all is said and done, many possibilities of other interpretations remain open. That is why I said that of course I did not maintain that one cannot be an intelligent Christian and continue to believe in a bodily resurrection.

For myself I find these historical arguments quite compelling; but my fundamental reason for basing my Easter sermon on the appearances of Jesus, and not on the empty tomb, is not historical but religious. It is a double reason. First, that sight, or objective proof, is not the proper ground of faith; and I think that the passionate desire of many of my correspondents to cling to the historicity of the empty tomb is due to a failure to realize this truth. Secondly, that I believe that Christ's Resurrection is the assurance that we too shall rise from the dead. I think that this implies that his Resurrection was not different in kind from what we may hope for through him; that our rising will be a

---

[1] The speeches in Acts are, in my view, reliable evidence for the way in which Luke, and the church in which he wrote, understood the gospel, but not for the original preaching of Peter and the other apostles.

sharing in that Resurrection. Further, the truth of the Incarnation is that the Son of God became fully man. He entered into our human condition, and experienced all that belongs to our human nature, without the sin which is a perversion of our nature (but not, of course, without temptation, which does belong to it). This means that he experienced the whole course of our life from birth to the grave and whatever lies beyond it. Yet, if his body was raised physically from the grave and did not see corruption, or if his body was transformed after death into something different, in such a way that in itself it was annihilated, then he did not experience the whole of our human destiny. His entry into life beyond the grave was different from what we hope may be our own. For it is demonstrable that our bodies of flesh and blood will be dissolved, and that in whatever mode of existence we may be raised from death it will not be by either the resuscitation of this mortal body or its transformation—unless, indeed, we follow the speculations of some of the Fathers concerning the reassembling, by God, of the dispersed molecules of the flesh, which I am not inclined to do.

The lines of Baxter's well-known hymn have been a source of hope and comfort at countless funerals.

> Christ leads me through no darker rooms
> Than he went through before;
> He that into God's kingdom comes
> Must enter by this door.

But if the story of the empty tomb were true, Christ's door into God's kingdom would not be ours. We should be confronted by another door through which he has never entered: into a dark room which his incarnate presence has never lightened.

For it is the Resurrection alone that gives us sure hope of a life to come. In my sermon I said that there is nothing inherent in our own nature on which we can rely for our hope; nothing, as it were, whether we call it a soul or anything else, which provides us with a built-in guarantee of survival. We believe that we shall live after death, not because of anything in ourselves, but because the God who raised Jesus is our Father, because he is unchanging, and because his love for us does not change, even, as the Resurrection assures us, through death. The principle of our immortality, if we may call it that, is God's relationship to us which he has established by grace. It is this relationship which, we may believe, overcomes death. Of course, if my relationship to God continues, then I must continue: as my self, or my soul (I take these terms as synonymous), not in this present bodily mode of existence, but living because the God on whom my life depends will maintain his grace towards me. I do not mean that my existence will depend on whether, or how firmly, I believe in God through Christ; but that it must depend on the love of God through Christ for me. This does not imply that this bodily existence is of only limited value or importance; the value of the material creation does not necessarily involve its eternity. For us, as the only mode of existence we know, and as the mode which God has seen to be good, it is of supreme value and importance. Yet it may be transcended by the relationship of God to us in which he has made us his sons; and it is that sonship which assures us of life beyond death even though the mode of that life is entirely beyond our imagination.

5

THE RESURRECTION

A MEDITATION

D. M. MacKinnon

As Professor Lampe says in his introduction, among those who criticized his broadcast and whose criticisms gave rise to the foregoing statement, was his colleague, Professor MacKinnon. His approach to the significance of the Resurrection is expressed in a meditation broadcast in the Third Programme as long ago as 1953—'that memorable broadcast,' as Professor Howard Root described it at the beginning of his own Third Programme Meditation of 1966.

THE RESURRECTION

A MEDITATION

D. M. MacKinnon

I suppose that there are people for whom the Resurrection of Christ presents no problem. Those, on the one hand, for whom it is a fable; those for whom, on the other, it is, as they say, 'the best attested fact in human history'. The former ignore it, and the latter can argue happily for its reality. Both are at home with it, whether they affirm it or whether they deny it. It is an event which did or did not happen.

But if we go beyond those points of view, what then? The Gospel records are short enough, never easy, but seeming hardly at first sight to support a weight of dogmatic construction. The references in the Epistles are frequent, but they are often elusive and difficult: where, indeed, do they take us?

Now, let us be fair. The Gospel writers do make clear that on Easter Day events happened which were qualitatively similar to previous events. The morning itself comes thirty-six hours after Christ died upon the Cross: women prepare to anoint his body, and so on. The continuities are there of space and time. Moreover, it remains true that either the tomb was found empty or it was not. What, then, is wrong with the simple down-to-earth realism of those who say that either Christ rose or he did not? Simply, I think, that they would enclose within the category of event what is itself more than event. Was there, then, no night which, in the words of the Paschal hymn, saw Christ 'rise again from hell'? Certainly; but that resurrection, although in one sense in time, possesses also a relation to the eternal as ultimate and unique as that of the universe itself to its creation. Indeed, what I would be prepared to argue is that here for Christians is focused the very relation of the temporal to the eternal itself. So that maybe we would not be wrong if we saw creation itself through this event, which is more than event. All this the Gospels make clear. The economy of their narrative (in Mark perhaps only eight verses) aids us to a proper perspective. We are never allowed to be obsessed by thaumaturgical detail or distracted by idle curiosity. It is as if here was something crucial, indeed determinative of the whole narrative of the life of Jesus: something whose import we grasp if we see that life anew in its light.

Thus the Resurrection plunged the disciples back into meditation on the things they had seen and heard. But this meditation was altogether free from nostalgic longing for what was past. The old comradeship on the road and in the street, in the house and at the supper table, was gone. But what had been present in those events, what indeed, they had gone to shape, that abided.

The life of Jesus belonged, indeed, to the ordinary world; the world of Caiaphas and Pilate, the world of zealots and Pharisees. Like all that belongs to that world, it made a tale that men could tell; like all that belonged to that world it moved from life to death; only more rapidly than in the case of many men. But when he rose his life rose with him. The impact that he had made on his friends became no longer a thing of transient force; but their memories of what they had witnessed were held firm even as their imaginations were quickened to ever deepening insight; into the eternal setting of the simplest human occasion of Christ's life.

Thus the Resurrection did not provoke men to speculative dreams concerning the hereafter, or even to argument that it had really happened. Rather, it mattered so much that almost it did not matter. Through it they saw anew the things that had been.

'Lord, thou knowest my downsitting and mine uprising.' These words from the 139th Psalm are traditionally used as the Introit for the Mass of Easter Day. Their suggestion is plain: it is not only the prince of this world who came to sift Christ in the hour of his Passion: it was the Father also who in him found no fault at all. The language of the Introit sees the Passion as a kind of judgement through which Christ passed, and in which he was acquitted. His fidelity in that hour was supremely tested, but it remained unimpaired. He was obedient unto death. So, in the language of Scripture, 'his Father raises him'.

'His Father raises him.' What do these words mean? They indicate the ultimate mystery of which one can only speak in metaphor; when, for instance, one speaks of the Resurrection as the Father's Amen to the work of Christ. But that Amen is not word; it is deed. For he is raised. And by his Resurrection an eternity is bestowed upon his work. *Tetelestai; Consummatum est.* According to the Fourth Evangelist this was his last word upon the Cross as he received the vinegar before he gave up the ghost. And that, his finished work, abides. By the Resurrection the very stuff of Christ's self-oblation perfected in death is given a universal contemporaneity. More, it becomes the ultimate context of all our lives.

'Christ being raised from the dead dieth no more; death has no more dominion over him.' So St Paul. If Christ lives now, his life no longer moves to the horizon of death; it is life absolute and unconfined. But its stuff, its very substance, is what in the days of his flesh was expressed in a relentless movement from Galilee to Jerusalem, from life to death. And on our own lives, as they too know the rhythm of that journey, it sets the seal of its own perfection.

But what does this mean? If you ask me, all I can say is that I am speaking here of what I think lies at the heart of the Christian understanding of the world. To the Christian the world is brought into a new and abiding relationship to God by the work of Christ. Note these last words: for what I am speaking of is something which was really worked out.

For the Christian as much as for the Marxist[1] there is a sense in which deed takes precedence over idea; or rather, idea is significant only as expressed in action. By the obedience of the second Adam the children of the first Adam are redeemed, and, I repeat, that obedience was worked out. No writing in the New Testament brings this out more clearly than the Fourth Gospel; the Gospel that some of the Fathers called the 'Spiritual Gospel'. The agony in Gethsemane is not recorded by this evangelist, inasmuch as he would rather show the whole life of Jesus as a waiting upon God the Father. Jesus is, indeed, presented in St John as one who of himself can do or say nothing at all: who is always waiting upon an hour that is not yet, as if he were the slave of a destiny not in his own power. But, of course, this servitude is presented as loving obedience to his Father. So, paradoxically, he says that no man takes his life from him; but he lays it down of himself.

There is no contradiction here, for he and his Father are one. At the heart of human history, then, stands for the Christian the agony, the struggle of Christ; this mysterious

---

[1] In a short article written by request for the monthly *Marxism Today* (the theoretical and discussion journal of the Communist Party of Great Britain) and published in the June 1966 number (pp. 186–187) as a contribution to the British dialogue between Christianity and Marxism, corresponding to that already going on in Eastern Europe, I refer again to this very important point of agreement between Christians and Marxists over against e.g. the disguised idealism encouraged under the label existentialism. Here I find nothing in the broadcast which I wish to modify!

and awful patience of his which yet seems big with inexhaustible energy of mercy and compassion. It is deed: not idea. So that we know that 'where death arose, thence life rose again; and that power which by a tree once vanquished us was on a tree brought low'. The demonic strength of egoism which we know in ourselves was powerless to bring Christ down. For himself he asked nothing at all—and on the Cross in his self-abandon he revealed himself to men as the Son of God, one who is, in the depths of his being, eternally response to the Father and nothing else. Yet these things were most painfully done. Revelation is not in a charade but in an agony, with flesh racked with pain, and human consciousness lost in sense of the meaninglessness of the world.

I say that on the Cross Christ revealed himself as the Son of God. Such, indeed, is the word of St Mark who makes the Centurion's avowal the climax of his Passion narrative. St Mark, whose narrative of the Resurrection is so strangely short, ending, it would seem, with the flight of the women from the tomb, finds the great climax in the Centurion's avowal, because he can look back upon the Cross in the light of the Resurrection. He is not so far from the Fourth Evangelist, whose sense of the mystery is so great that he consistently presents the Cross as glory and exaltation: the throne from which the Son of Man judged the world. Luke, in a lesser way, presents the last journey to Jerusalem as a triumphal progress, its end to be an *analempsis*, an assumption.

All this should help us to see what in one sense the Resurrection is. It is the raising of the whole life and death of Christ to a place where men can see it, as the merciful act of God's love. There is far more in the Gospels about the Resurrection than the actual resurrection narratives I mentioned a little while back. In a way, and not in Luke only, the whole presentation of the Via Crucis is a witness and an interpretation of the Resurrection. The approach of

Christ to his Passion is seen as an element in the total mystery of Jesus; with whom the believer is contemporary. And that mystery is a thing of joy. In the Western liturgy of Good Friday, suddenly and almost unexpectedly, the rhythm of penitence is broken by the words, 'We venerate thy Cross, O Lord, and praise and glorify thy holy Resurrection, because by virtue of that Cross joy has come to the whole world'. There's a similar interweaving there to the one I've just spoken of in the Gospels.

But, of course, the Resurrection is not simply interpretation. It is deed, even as the Passion is deed. Called deed, I think, by analogy. Just as we speak of it as event and yet not event, so we speak of it as deed and yet not deed. For in this action the agent is the eternal God who raises Jesus from the dead. I spoke a while back of the relation of the Resurrection to the Father as being as ultimate and unique as that of creation itself. But then, you may remember, I was careful to qualify myself. It is indeed the relation of the creation to God that is illuminated by this awful mystery. We cannot see the relation, either of history or of nature, to the Father, except across the mystery of the Resurrection of Christ. Our thought of creation is rescued from abstraction when we see its fulfilment in the tomb of Christ, the birthplace of his glory, and the glory of his own.

'The Paschal mystery is the fundamental Christian mystery.' So, recently, a Continental theologian, thinking perhaps primarily of sacraments as the means whereby human life is knit into the fabric of Christ's dying and arising. But the words have wider senses than that. Here, in the Resurrection, all the problems of theology are raised; for here revelation makes its ultimate claim: the claim that the Redeemer is Lord at once of history and of nature. The manner of his Lordship is patience and mercy. It is achieved, indeed expressed, in obedience unto death. But none the less in the mystery of his Resurrection he is revealed as Lord.

His patience is shown as powerful to the overcoming of death itself, and his mercy shown in the hour of his awful triumph to those who failed him is now shown to men as a final mercy. In the presence of Christ's Resurrection we are in the presence of the final things of God, of victory, not as the world knows it, but as God knows it, in the subduing of all things to the purposes of his mercy. What we are met with here we can perhaps only show in a half light; but its claim remains to ultimacy and finality.

Can these things be? To some, all that I have said must seem absurd. Certainly, we have to do with what in the nature of the case can only be a matter of revelation. For such, of course, the story of Jesus claims to be, and in one sense the Resurrection is almost identifiable with this claim that it is revelation itself. For how could a life be the revelation of God? Surely, only if in it were focused the dealings of God with men. And, of course, men have found that the way of Jesus, the way through death to Resurrection, illuminates, if it does not wholly condition, their spiritual lives. We know, most of us, what it is to be broken; to shed, at least, some of the illusions we have about ourselves, and we know that these moments can be a kind of death; a death, too, that we must accept: for only as we accept it, as we go down into it, can we find renewal, or rather, be overtaken by the renewing hand of God. And these deaths, of course, speak to us of our own bodily death which will surely come, perhaps cutting across our life's work before it is even half ended, leaving loose ends in every direction. We must die. Perhaps we look to survival, perhaps the dynamism of our thought and choice seems to evidence the immortal in us. But again, in a behaviourist age the autonomy of spirit is a more precarious belief than it was in the heyday of metaphysical idealism.

In a way, as I think I have said, the Resurrection of Jesus can be seen as the revelation of the nature of his dying. He died the death of a criminal, the death of the cursed. On the other hand, he imposed upon his execution the style of self-oblation. This he did in the Upper Room when he invested his death with sacrificial significance. He makes of his judicial murder an ultimate act of homage and reparation to his Father. He took the ghastly business of dying and converted it into an act of wholly obedient love. He died, and he was raised.

And in his death he gathers the dying of men into that his archetypal self-surrender. Of their deaths he makes a part of his abiding prayer. Does this seem morbid and fanciful? It is, I think, an aspect of the joy which through the Cross of Christ has come into the world: this refusal to ignore the extremities of human existence, but to find in them the stuff of praise. Our death is not simply something through which we pass. It is become through Christ an act; it is certainly the term of life and beyond it lies the secret way of purification on which Christ guides his own. But it is also in itself the gathering up of life in final homage to God. For he it is who gives and takes away. And if we make of our very incompleteness, of the fragmentary brokenness of our lives, of which death is the most eloquent sign, an act of love towards him, then assuredly we have lived and died in some understanding of the mystery of the Resurrection of Christ from the dead. 'In manus tuas, Domine, commendo animam meam.'

6

GOOD FRIDAY AND EASTER

AN INTERPRETATION

D. M. MacKinnon

Professor MacKinnon looks again at his Meditation and, in the light of it, considers Professor Lampe's statement.

6

GOOD FRIDAY AND EASTER

AN INTERPRETATION

D. M. MacKinnon

To RE-READ after an interval of more than a decade the preceding meditation is to be conscious of the extent to which my thinking on the topics with which it dealt has moved and has become much less confident, the outlines far less secure. In the meditation I was prepared to take a number of categories for granted which further reflection has led me to question: for instance, the notion of sacrifice that informed a part of what I then wrote.

I mention this concept of sacrifice in particular because if I have to ask wherein I still differ from Professor Lampe (whose consummate New Testament scholarship I would not venture to query), it touches the question of the unique and creative quality of Christ's work.

> Christ leads me through no darker rooms
> Than he went through before.

Baxter's hymn which Professor Lampe quotes is almost certainly among the greatest in the English language, and I do not question its relevance to the issue we are discussing. But what exactly do the words say? Surely that whatever experience may be ours, it is not to be regarded as in itself more terrible than Christ's Passion; it is not suggested that the dark experiences may not be quite different one from another.

Many years ago I recall hearing an address on Good Friday evening in which the preacher suggested to his congregation that it might fall to them in 'filling up what is lacking in the suffering of Christ for his Body's sake' to endure kinds of ill of whose occurrence in his brief human life we have no record, for instance, prolonged physical illness. To one facing the ordeal of cancer, awaiting, for instance, the passage of the common two years' interval between the appearance of the first malignant growth and its possible recrudescence, there may be consolation in the recollection of Christ's ordeal, but a consolation, the preacher implicitly argued, that need not be diminished by the sense that here is an experience which in a quite literal sense the Lord did not share. The argument of this sermon was open to criticism on the ground that the preacher seemed to take for granted a highly debatable view of the redemptive value of human suffering; yet he was calling attention to something very important, namely, that if we quote Baxter's words as Professor Lampe has done, we must not forget that the scope of Christ's suffering is limited. It included extremities of human pain; but it was not the only sort of ordeal that overtakes humankind.

Again one thinks of the monstrous indignities of the geriatric wards of a modern hospital, of the fantasies of the senile, of the disintegration typified by the onset of double incontinence. No one who has had one whom he loved die in such straits will fail to welcome the compassionate realism of the graveside prayer, 'Suffer us not at the last from any pains of death to fall from thee'. In the original of Isaac Watts' hymn, it was the 'young Prince of Glory' who died on Calvary, forgoing most certainly opportunities of profound service to his fellows that might well have been his, had he avoided the issue of his supreme hour. But we must not let our proper embarrassment at the unfeeling vulgarity of, e.g., the notorious Armistice hymn, 'The Supreme Sacrifice', lead us to forget that death in youth at least spares the one who dies the degeneration which so often today marks the way to the tomb.

On Easter Day, 1962 (April 22nd), Mr. Kingsley Amis, the novelist, published in the *Sunday Telegraph* an article in which he tried to formulate his attitude to the central figure of the Gospels. He, rightly in my judgement, remarked that one of the aspects of his life which seemed to set a question-mark against his claim was the fact that he avoided what for very many, if not most, men is the most testing of all human experiences, viz. marriage and the begetting of children. Here lies not only the most inexorable of all human responsibilities, but here as nowhere else men are revealed to themselves as what they are, tested and unmasked. Here is, no doubt, a place of glory, but for others also the setting of their most tragic experience, and first-hand knowledge of failure and despair. 'The Son of Man had not where to lay his head.' Such rootlessness protects its subject from human demands even as it exposes him to the pains of homelessness. Those who know from within what marriage may demand are often unimpressed with the claim of the celibate that his way of life is renunciation for the service of the higher good, even when it is conceded to be innocent altogether of any unconscious homosexuality. Those who have suffered through marriage or even known its average demands, are aware of the foot-loose ease that rejection of its responsibilities confers and are unwilling to see here nothing but renunciation. And what is validly brought in criticism against the devoted monk in the mission field must surely have a *prima facie* relevance to the Lord himself.

The point is a very important one, and it can only be met if we can show that Christ was by the nature of his mission constrained to accept certain limitations, this because only by doing so could he fulfil a task, the task which touches the heart and centre of human life. What I dare to query in Professor Lampe's argument is a bias in the direction of exemplarism; this though he insists that the Resurrection of Christ has much more than a purely cognitive significance. It may indeed seem that what I have done so far is to offer a tentative argument against the claims of an exemplarist interpretation of Christ's work, namely, that if he is offered us as an exemplar his experience is in crucial respects too relative and limited to offer a wholly significant guide-post to men and women in all the circumstances of their lives. This, of course, is not to say he is not rightly esteemed truly human, a man of flesh and blood with the peculiar Biblical force of that phrase; indeed it might be claimed that the very stress laid on the limited character of his experience makes us more vividly aware of the reality of his human nature. Yet we need to recognize the problems raised for us by the fact that if his limitation emphasizes his humanity, it is expressed in a deliberate selection from the range of activities open to him, such a selection indeed as men and women are always compelled to make. For him as for others choice closed some doors even as it opened others. Yet the doors which he was content should remain closed were among the most significant confronting humankind, and if we are to vindicate his readiness that they should so remain sealed, we can only do so if we suppose that his mission imposed on him a particular set of choices.

Where an understanding of the Resurrection of Christ is concerned, historical, philosophical and theological problems are inextricably intertwined. But they do not concern simply the relative lateness of the emergence of the empty tomb tradition; they concern much more Christ's approach to his Passion, the intention with which he confronted his supreme hour. In what sense do we regard the Cross as an act creative in itself, as an *opus operatum* whose agent in the loneliness of his total rejection achieved something new, radically affected the scheme of things entire, established in respect of the relations of men and women to God a new foundation?

Or are we, partly by the paucity of our records, whose composition has been so largely shaped by factors quite other than a modern demand for historical, factual accuracy, partly by the demands of a theology that would emphasize divine acceptance above divine judgement, compelled to say that all we find here is the most sublime presentation in time of the eternal readiness of God to receive to himself the truly penitent? In my meditation it was to the former view that I was committed; I would not now use confidently the almost liturgical language I made free with them. I would try rather to say at least a considerable part of what I said then in a very different way.

Consider this passage from a Cambridge philosopher:[1]

But though we do make and need to make limited judgements we need again and again to call to mind how different they are from the divine judgement in which both easy forgiveness and easy condemnation are impossible. This is the judgement we ask for ourselves. For we ask that at our own trial counsel and judge shall proceed with infinite patience. We ask that they shall not judge a part of the picture without seeing the whole. We ask that they shall consider, ruthlessly but with understanding, circumstance beyond circumstance, wheel within wheel.

Asking for this patience for ourselves we then ask it for others and so ask it of ourselves.

Is it not an element in Christian belief that in the Passion of Christ precisely that marriage of truth and justice with mercy which Professor Wisdom seems to desiderate was achieved? Wisdom is writing of the human situation, and we must not suppose that if we agree with what he writes, we are assuming a schism between God's justice and his mercy. What we are supposing and implying is that in our heart of hearts we ask for what seems beyond possibility of bestowal, a judgement that neither spares our capacity for self-deceit in respect of our selves and our relationships,

[1] Professor John Wisdom, *Paradox and Discovery*, Blackwell, 1966, p. 33.

nor annihilates the springs of our tenderness towards our neighbours and indeed towards ourselves.

Where the understanding of Christ's Passion is concerned we are, as always, involved inextricably in historical questions of great difficulty. In the Synoptic Gospels the framework of the narrative is in a measure provided by the movement of the Lord from Galilee to Jerusalem, from life to death. The earliest of the three (St Mark) is clearly the work of a writer almost obsessed by the apologetic necessity of somehow making intelligible to his readers the scandalous outcome in rejection and death of the ministry of one whom he clearly believed to be the expected Messiah. The very depth of his preoccupation with the theological problem presented by the terrible fate meted out to Jesus as a result of the Jewish and Roman leaders' readiness to co-operate in his destruction makes him a questionable witness to the motives and intentions with which the Lord approached and confronted his supreme hour. In the very different narrative of St Luke we are continually reminded that a triumphal progress, begun when the day of Christ's assumption was near, provides the (artificial) context of many of the events he records. The movement from Nazareth to Galilee is followed by one from Galilee to Jerusalem; and in his sequel, the Acts of the Apostles, the Evangelist will continue the progress to Rome itself. Again, if the writer of the Fourth Gospel radically departs from the topographical scheme of his predecessors, his whole presentation is dominated by references to an hour 'that is not yet come', but which controls and directs by its ever hastening approach the sequence of events he sets forth.

There is no escaping the extreme difficulty that confronts any attempt to frame a doctrine of the Atonement as a result of the growing recognition of the extent to which motives of theological and apologetic construction determine the Gospels as we have them. Yet suppose we allow ourselves for a moment to attend to the Lucan portrait of the central figure. An intelligible portrait certainly emerges of one who of fixed intention consorts with the socially and morally outcast in preference to the religious and moral élite of the society in which he lived and acted. It is indeed arguable that the order in which Luke sets out the temptations of Christ sets the tone for his presentation of his ministry. The climactic temptation is not the offer of the kingdoms of the world and their glory, but the suggestion of a bloodless victory achieved by a miraculous descent upon the central scene of devotion and worship. Such a descent would immediately set its subject alongside those concerned to promote authoritatively the cause of religion and morals, and establish an immediate gulf between him and those of whom he spoke as 'the lost sheep of Israel'. Certainly Luke's Christ is one who follows to the end the way of presence, repudiating at the last the challenge to descend from the Cross, preferring to keep company to the end with the thief whose stumbling confession of his lordship Luke includes in his Passion-narrative. Yet a student of this portrait must ask himself how such association is possible, how it may be pursued without risk of corruption to the one who attempts it, without indeed risk of perpetuating a kind of deceit concerning the way of life adopted by those who are thus made welcome by Christ. No one who knows anything of the darker side of human life will deny that acceptance in itself can pass easily into a sentimental condonation of evil which obscures the truth of human existence. A father who welcomes home his prodigal son must be careful lest in his old age he become a Lear, easy prey to the flatteries of a Goneril or Regan, blind to the devotion of a Cordelia and unable until almost too late to find healing for his fantasies in her fidelity to the truth. It is indeed part of the depth of Christ's parables, and of his own ministry seen as

in itself the supreme parable, that they point beyond themselves. The parable of the two brothers is full of the ambiguity
of human life; its ending is not the happy ending which
closes for ever the issues with which it deals. It points beyond
itself. So analogously does the ministry of Jesus. Luke sets it
forth as the actualization of a sustained choice of acceptance;
but it is an acceptance by one whose face is set steadfastly
to go to Jerusalem, a triumphant progress indeed but one
suffused by a resolution that can only be indicated by use
of the active (*esterixen*) of that verb used in the perfect passive
in the parable of Dives and Lazarus to convey the gulf
between Heaven and Hell.

The depths of human ambiguity are opened and plumbed
by Christ himself. Such seems to me to be part of the burden
of the Johannine theological sequel to the Synoptic narratives, as well as of those narratives themselves. To plumb
these depths he gave himself in obedience to his Father; he so
lived that he opened to the seemingly fathomless bottom
the central contradiction of human existence, the inescapable
conflict of the claims of love and truth. We can surely read
off from the Gospels something of the cost of this, something
indeed of the uncertainty that hemmed his choice; the out-
rage of the Pharisees, the seeming desertion at the last of the
common people who had heard him gladly and whom in a
sense he left to their fate in the coming sack of their city
and desolation of their land. One can even discern the
stamp of the homelessness to which his being as 'the man for
God' condemned him, on his ministry from the beginning.
Yet it is more than a stamp; it is a burden laid upon him
which makes him wholly acceptable, vulnerable, *disponible*,
and yet withdraws him to the task of 'giving his flesh for
the life of the world': almost in the moment when an outburst
of popular devotion would bestow upon him the splendour
of kingship, a kingship of popular acclaim which he refused

without seeming even to consider attempting to manage it. The very possibility of such status is presented by John as intractable by one whose destiny it is to be presented in the end to the world as Son of Man, with mock robes of royalty upon him, to pick out the unique dignity and situation of the one by whom the world is finally judged. Because it is intractable he simply dodges the kingship of acclaim, awaiting instead the coronation that will be his in his supreme hour, a coronation which by its quality of contempt suggests, even partially reveals, the many-levelled mystery of the Son of Man.

Of course this is not a doctrine of the Atonement. It is at best a prolegomenon which seeks to suggest an element in the ministry of Jesus that gives it a constitutive as distinct from an exemplary character, that makes it the supreme action of all history (action that is fully and entirely human, yet unique), action which crowns a ministry in which the ambiguities of human life are progressively articulated, being action in which their burden is endured *à l'outrance*.

In his recently published book, *According to Your Faith*, Mr T. S. Gregory, who produced the meditation when it was broadcast in 1953, wrote as follows: 'The Cross is Love without remorse or reprieve, sovereign and everlasting, the sole image of omnipotence known to me'.[1] This is a wholly admirable statement of the revelation of the ways of God with men that is afforded to their perceptions in Christ's Cross. By this event they are enabled, even compelled, radically to redefine their notion of his sovereign power as it affects their lives; but if they are allowed in that place to glimpse the ultimate secret of his ways, this would seem in part at least to be because there he made, in the person of his Son, their perplexity and their pain his own. We are brought face to face here with some of the deepest intellectual

[1] Op. cit., p. 108.

problems, and indeed most searching spiritual mysteries of
the Christian faith, namely the manner of our dependence on
God in Christ and the detail, so far as we can trace it, of
God's dealing with us in him. If writing a technical philosophical or theological essay, I should wish here to urge how
much work needs to be done by way of analysis on the notion
of dependence.[1] What do we mean when we speak of our
dependence on God? Further, what did, for instance, the
late Dom Gregory Dix, in the last and most permanently
valuable chapter of his *Shape of the Liturgy*,[2] mean when he
said that 'we depend upon God for our very dependence'?
He was speaking of that which he saw articulated in the
Catholic tradition of Eucharistic worship, as he understood
it; yet his words unconsciously echoed a great deal that is
most deeply characteristic of Dr Karl Barth's criticism of
what he regards as the very heart and centre of Catholic
dogmatics, namely the doctrine of the analogy of being.
These are matters as technical as they are difficult; yet the
attempt to present in the simplest, I had almost said most
naked, terms the elements of the Christian faith raises them
very sharply. It is a paradox, yet true, that the more deeply
we seek to affirm the reality of God's condescension to the
depths of our human situation, the more we are enabled,
and indeed led, somehow to represent the content of his act
in Christ in objective terms. This is not to deny for one
moment what Mr Gregory has recently written with such
authoritative perception; rather it is to say that the Cross
only reveals the secret of the divine ways because it is dealing
with men and women as they are.

It is currently fashionable to write as if the very heart and
centre of the Christian gospel was a simple message of divine
acceptance. This is a very healthy corrective to a great deal

[1] In the second series of my Gifford Lectures delivered in Edinburgh, I include
(especially in the version to be published) extended discussion of this notion.
[2] Dacre Press (1945).

that has unquestionably disfigured the history of institutional Christianity; for instance, the sometimes subtle but persistent belittling of the richest and most profound of human experiences, as if the joys of *human* love were somehow suspect, and not among the most sheerly precious experiences that life has to offer. But the message of divine acceptance is sometimes presented as an ultimately sentimental underwriting of every sort of self-indulgence, disregard of the claims of others, cruelty and self-deception, as if everything, but everything, was for the best in the best of all possible worlds. The deadliness of what Plato referred to as the 'lie in the soul', succeeding in no small measure in characterizing its inwardness, is too lightly dismissed. We rightly reject the sort of spiritual shallowness which expresses itself in an affected superiority in the presence of the extraordinary richness of human life, that underplays the wonder and the joy of married love, and at the same time (there is a connection) depreciates the worlds of natural beauty and of the arts. But we could too easily replace this shallowness by another, cruel as sentimental attitudes inevitably are, which leaves out of account the presence in human life of the sheerly irrevocable, of that which has been done, and it is now too late to undo, of the damage inflicted on others that cannot be put right and that no interpretation can possible render edifying. It is such considerations as these that have weighed with those who have insisted that the atoning work of Christ must be construed in objective terms, who have indeed sometimes found themselves driven by recollection of the Cross to give this temper to their humanism.

I may seem to have moved a long way from the issues with which this discussion is primarily concerned. Yet I agree with Professor Lampe profoundly in thinking that no simple treatment of the Resurrection narratives is possible. I mean they are not capable of allowing us the comfort of a simple yes or no to what they imply. I will not deny that I give more weight than he does to the fact of the apparent inability of the opponents of the early Christian preaching to silence the message of the Resurrection once for all by producing Christ's remains. The account we have of this preaching in *Acts* raises every sort of historical critical problem, and I would not pretend to any knowledge in depth of the issues involved. But there seems to me at the common-sense level something here that we must take seriously, more seriously than any other element in the traditional Easter apologetic. Yet when that is said and done the narratives need to be studied not only in the closest detail but also in relation to the whole problem of Christ's person and work. If we say that we suppose the sense of that work to reside in the end in a definitive declaration of the ways of God with men, made in man for men, we will, I suspect, incline towards a view that diminishes the element of uniqueness we attribute to Christ's Resurrection. If, on the other hand, we suppose something done here once for all, we will not be surprised to find in the manner of the Amen spoken to that work an element of the unique. I say an element of the unique; for clearly there is some sort of analogy between the content of the Christian hope and the manner of Christ's raising from the dead. Again we are brought up against the obscurities attending the use here of the notion of dependence. How does that for which we hope, however uncertainly and precariously, depend upon that which Christ received as vindication of his work? This is a matter on which there is most urgent need of co-operation between those whose studies are, in the first instance, historical, and those whose concern lies on the frontiers between systematic theological understanding and the clamant need to relate the supposed Christian verity to our growing and changing perceptions of our human situation. I say this because I realize that in what I have written it is not simply a matter of a dogmatic theologian commenting on the work of a disciplined historical critic; there are issues involved here which are neither purely theological nor historical; they touch the manner in which we understand our existence and our need, an existence and an understanding that we allow it possible that Christ has redefined for us. But what is the manner, what the secret, of that redefinition? Here, as so often when one really tries to get to grips with the Christian message, its articulation in hard and fast terms seems to elude us; we are pulled in a whole number of directions at once, no more able to say simply that here we deal with historical questions, here with questions of general philosophy or of human psychology, here with matters of revealed theology. It is almost as if we have here a kind of dependence that deprives us of the sort of security that we tend uncritically to associate with a dependence for which we claim ultimacy. We are left asking questions in a process of interrogation that is partly, though not entirely, self-interrogation, to which we see no easy end; but this may be as it is because the mysteries that set our inquiring in motion have their authority over us, thus continually to disturb our minds, only because they do touch what is ultimate, which is at once within and yet wholly beyond our comprehension.

It may seem odd to end these comments with what may seem to many needless epistemological obscurities; but I am driven to write in these terms because I sometimes think that only when we bring out into the open what it is that defeats our every attempt to handle the things of the Christian faith confidently and without hesitation, will we be able to perceive at least a small measure of its uniqueness. There is, perhaps, no place at which these issues are more sharply raised than consideration of the gospel of the Resurrection.

7

A REJOINDER

G. W. H. Lampe

As the dialogue progresses, Professor Lampe looks back at his own statement on Easter in the light of Professor MacKinnon's Meditation and of his interpretation of the Resurrection.

7

A REJOINDER

G. W. H. Lampe

PROFESSOR MACKINNON'S broadcast meditation recalls us from the question, 'What happened at Easter?', to the much more important and profound subject of what it means to us to believe that God has raised Jesus from the dead. I greatly welcome this turn in the discussion, for this latter question was also the theme of my own sermon, and it was only because the former arose in 'Meeting Point' and was seized upon by many of my correspondents that I have had to devote a disproportionate amount of space to the historical problem. My object in preaching was, in fact, to enunciate in less sophisticated language precisely that truth which Professor MacKinnon expresses when he says: 'Here in the Resurrection . . . revelation makes its ultimate claim; the claim that the Redeemer is Lord at once of history and of nature. The manner of his Lordship is patience and mercy. It is achieved, indeed expressed, in obedience unto death. But none the less in the mystery of his Resurrection he is revealed as Lord. His patience is shown as powerful to the overcoming of death itself, and his mercy, shown in the hour of his awful triumph to those who failed him, is now shown to men as a final mercy. In the presence of Christ's Resurrection we are in the presence of the final things of God, of victory, not as the world knows it, but as God knows it, in the subduing of all things to the purposes of his mercy. What we are met with here we can perhaps only show in a half light; but its claim remains to ultimacy and finality.'

This is wholly true. The Resurrection is an enigma, in the sense that no one is, or ever has been, able to comprehend the manner in which God raised Jesus from the dead. But it is the decisive event in the history of the world: the focal point in God's dealings with his creation. The Resurrection placed the human life of Christ in the perspective of eternity. It could now be seen, in every detail as his followers remembered it, as the life of the one whom they now encountered as a living Presence in the witnessing and worshipping life of the Christian society: the Jesus who was no longer with them as 'the prophet from Nazareth', but who was for ever contemporary as the Lord to whom 'all authority in heaven and earth' had been given, who was 'with them always, to the close of the age'. The Resurrection made it possible to look back upon that human life with fresh insight, so that in later years St John could write a Gospel in which, though the subject is still the events which took place in Galilee and Jerusalem, the deeds and words of Jesus are reinterpreted in the full light of his risen glory. The true meaning of what he had done and said, which could scarcely be understood by those who were eyewitnesses at the time, was now revealed as the Holy Spirit brought to the remembrance of his disciples all that he had said, and guided them into all the truth (Jn. 14. 26, 16. 13). And in this new perspective Jesus was seen to be himself the ultimate truth: the very embodiment of God's Word. In him they saw how things really are; they saw that in all the universe the central fact and the sovereign power is the love which shone out in him, the love by which they found themselves judged, forgiven, able to be re-created so as to become new people. Here, in the risen Lord, they discerned the meaning of Creation: 'The whole universe has been created through him and for him'. Here also they found the pledge and the anticipation of the ultimate completion of God's purpose for humanity: the re-making of mankind in unbroken fellowship with the Creator, refashioned according to the pattern of Jesus Christ.

There are points in Professor MacKinnon's meditation which I might wish to express somewhat differently. In particular, I should hesitate to adopt without some further explanation the idea that the Passion was 'a kind of judgement through which Christ passed, and in which he was acquitted'. I do not think that my difficulty arises from what Professor MacKinnon himself intends by this statement; and I could certainly gloss it in a way which would make me able to accept it. But I think there is some risk that it might be misconstrued so as to obscure certain truths which I believe to be fundamental: that the Passion is the moment at which that complete oneness with the Father which is the unique and all-pervading characteristic of the life of Jesus is paradoxically manifested; that it is at that moment, above all, that Jesus discloses to us God himself in action; that the judgement passed on Jesus and the testing brought to bear upon him are a judgement and a testing exercised (of course, within the permissive will of God) by evil men, or, to use mythological language, by the devil; and that the judgement of God pronounced at Calvary is that which Christ's accepting love passes upon those men, and upon ourselves as sharers in their sinfulness, by showing up their sin in all its hatefulness.

The meaning of the Cross, however, and its relation to the Resurrection, are discussed more fully in Professor Mac-Kinnon's comments, and, since my reaction to his Meditation as a whole is one of agreement and gratitude, I now turn to two particularly interesting points which he brings forward in his 'interpretation'.

The first concerns the uniqueness of Christ's work, and the bearing which this has upon the relation between his

Resurrection and our hope that we ourselves shall be raised from death by the grace of God who brought him again from the dead. That the Word of God was truly made man is the heart of the gospel. God Incarnate entered into our condition. He experienced life as we know it, and underwent our death. The central theme of the Epistle to the Hebrews is that he was made like us in all respects save for our sin; he calls us his brothers; in our humanity he is exalted to the throne of God, a high priest who is able to sympathize with our weaknesses. That he became man in order that we might be made sons of God, or be deified, is the often-repeated teaching of the Greek Fathers. The Son of God fully shared the lot of mortal men. Obviously, this cannot mean that he shared the whole range of human experience. That he took our nature upon him does not imply that every individual person, in every conceivable situation, has Christ as his forerunner and is following in his steps. The Incarnation necessarily involves particularity. If the Word was truly made flesh then he had to be incarnate as a certain individual man in a particular time and place. He was a first-century man, a Jew, a carpenter. His range of experience was restricted by the kind of man he was; and this in itself raises certain difficulties if he is held up as an example to all human beings everywhere and at all times, for it is at least in some measure unreal to present a first-century Galilean as a model for the conduct of Western or African or Asian men in a twentieth-century industrial society.

The significance of the Incarnation, however, is not that the life of Jesus constitutes an example for all subsequent human beings to follow in detail. It is rather that in the incarnation of the Word of God humanity has been taken into unity with God; human life has been sanctified; and a way has been opened for all men in every century and in all

circumstances to enter into their right relationship to the
Creator (the relationship of sons to their Father) through
God's gracious approach to them in Christ and the response
of trust and obedience which God in Christ evokes from them.
Entry into this relationship of grace and faith involves the
imitation of Christ, but this does not mean an imitation of
the individual pattern of life which was required of him by his
unique vocation; it means the imitation of his total commit-
ment to God, his obedience to God's will, and his attitude of
unswerving love for others which was the fruit of his open-
ness to God. In Jesus the creative Word of God does address
all men in their own situation, however different this may be
from the historical circumstances of his incarnate life. For
the life of each individual to be sanctified by that Word it is
not necessary that there should have been a myriad separate
incarnations.

It is true that Christians have rightly discerned in Jesus
the new, or second, Adam. In him they find man as God
intends him to be: man in the image of God, the perfection
of our humanity. He belongs to our race, sharing our pro-
pensities and temptations, bearing our human responsibilities
and enduring our human weakness; yet in him the sin of
Everyman, the inward-looking self-centredness which bars
the way to communion with God because it tries to establish
and justify itself over against God, is overcome. Adam's
eagerness to snatch the prize of equality with God—the
desire of Everyman to set himself up in the place of God as
absolute master of a world which is really not his own, but
God's—is replaced by the second Adam's total self-surrender:
his obedience to the point of accepting the death of the
Cross; death which paradoxically leads to life, whereas the
consequence of Adam's self-glorification proved to be death.
Christ is the second Adam, but only if he has fully entered
into, and fully transformed, the condition of Everyman.

All those experiences which necessarily fall to the lot of man must have been shared by him.

Marriage and parenthood, with the responsibilities, joys and sorrows which they entail, are not among those experiences which belong to man as such. Professor Mac-Kinnon is quite right to draw attention to the fact that here is a very large and most important sphere of human life which lay beyond the range of experience dictated by Jesus' particular calling. It is right to acknowledge that this gap in the human experience of the Word Incarnate causes difficulty to some people, for it seems on the surface that this most vital area of personal relationship and responsibility is to some extent a room which Christ has not been through before us. This means that the opportunities for direct imitation of Christ by us are correspondingly limited. Indeed, if the imitation of Christ is conceived in terms of a detailed reproduction of the actual manner in which he lived, the fact that he did not marry may have, and has had, serious consequences. It can constitute a ground for the notion that celibacy must form part of the ideal Christian life: the 'evangelical life' which the Church of the fourth and later centuries identified with monasticism. The result of this has sometimes been to misconceive the Christian virtue of chastity and distort it into an avoidance of personal responsibility in the centrally important areas of sex, married partnership and parenthood.

It is, however, as I have already argued, a fundamental mistake to interpret the *imitatio Christi* in this narrow fashion. The Christian is called, not to reproduce the externals of the life of Jesus, but to live in the spirit of Jesus: as St Paul would say, to know the indwelling presence of the Spirit whom God has sent into our hearts, by whom we can venture to call God 'Father'. We have to try to share Jesus' attitudes. It would, indeed, be a serious defect in his attitude to man if he had depreciated, or had no understanding of, marriage and parenthood, or if his life and teaching had been such as to have no relevance to married and family life. But this is far from the case. On the contrary, his sayings about marriage, his attitude to children, and the effect on his own thought of his early unrecorded home life, which is supremely evident in his attitude to God as Father and in his great parables of fatherhood, are of the most profound significance for married people at all times; and it was through reflection upon the divine love mediated by him to all men that the ancient picture of Israel as God's bride came to be applied in a new way, so as to make human marriage a fitting analogy to the risen Christ's communion with his people. 'The state of matrimony', as the Prayer Book puts it, has been 'consecrated to such an excellent mystery that in it is signified and represented the spiritual marriage and unity betwixt Christ and his Church.'

Old age, too, is an area of human experience which lies outside the immediate range of the Incarnation. Irenaeus seems to have felt this difficulty as he worked out the parallel between the second Adam and the first, and tried to show how the totality of human life had been taken up and transformed in the Incarnation; and it may strike us as rather absurd when he uses the saying of the Jews to Jesus, 'Thou art not yet fifty years old', as evidence that Jesus was in his forties at the time, and had thus reached an age which by ancient standards could be reckoned old. Yet although the geriatric ward as such is another 'darker room' than the one Christ actually went through, and though he was not called to face physical decay and senility, similar considerations are relevant here. Apart from the obvious fact that if Jesus had experienced the troubles of old age the Incarnation might have seemed of little relevance to those who are cut off in youth by violent death in battle or otherwise, old age, although a far more general condition in our time than ever before, is still not a part of the universal lot of man. It is not necessary to the completeness of the humanity of the second Adam that he should have suffered in this particular way, any more than that he should have experienced every kind of death that may befall us. On the other hand, Jesus did know many of the distresses that may afflict the aged; loneliness, poverty, abandonment, and, if the 'cry of dereliction' is to be taken in its full horror, as I think it should be, the extremity of physical weakness and mental dissolution. It is true for the old, as for the rest of us, that 'we have not a high priest who is unable to sympathize with our weaknesses'.

Those things, however, which inescapably belong to human existence as such are a different matter altogether. If the Word of God has entered into our condition in reality and not in mere appearance, he must have shared our birth. Hence there arises what I think is one of the major reasons why the miraculous birth recorded in Matthew and Luke should not be regarded as a historical fact but as a midrashic or mythical way of expressing the truth that the person of Christ cannot be understood exclusively within the dimension of humanity, but belongs also to the divine dimension. For it is apparent to us, as it was not to the ancients with their ignorance of genetics, that physical generation is involved in what it means to be 'man'; and Jesus is not a demi-god but the Son of God truly made man.

He must have been born. He must have grown up; and the value of Luke's emphasis on his 'increase in wisdom and stature' can be measured by the difficulty which this caused to later Christians who could not easily accept Christ's full manhood. He must have experienced death. No one, save some Docetist heretics, has doubted this; but the truth of it receives special emphasis, as I am inclined to think, in the inclusion of Jesus' actual burial in the very early tradition cited by Paul in 1 Corinthians 15. 4, and in the elaborate accounts by the Evangelists of the burial and of the size of the stone which barred the tomb.

He shared our human death; and I remain convinced that his entry into life beyond death was not dissimilar in its mode from ours. What may await us on the other side of death must not, if the Incarnation is real and Christ is the second Adam, be a room into which his presence has not preceded us. Unless we take an impossibly 'spiritualist' view of our human make-up, we cannot lightly contemplate the dissolution of the body without which we are unable, since we are physical beings, to conceive of a personality. Yet the dissolution of the body is most certainly part of the universal lot of man. I do not find it possible to believe that bodily corruption, that ultimate negation, as it seems, of all human endeavour, aspiration and hope, can be something from which the manhood of Christ was exempt. If God will raise us from death to a new life of fuller communion with himself, then this will be sheer miracle: God's re-creative Word affirming us in the moment of our utter nothingness. And if Christ is the firstfruits of the dead, his Resurrection cannot be of a different order from this. A Resurrection of his physical body, such as is implied by the empty tomb and by some of the stories in the Gospels of his appearances, would point towards a docetic Christ who does not fully share the lot of men; unless, indeed, bodily corruption were to be regarded as being bound up with the sinfulness of man which Christ did not share (but, unless we accept an impossibly literalistic interpretation of Genesis 3 as factual history, it is impossible to hold that physical dissolution is not part of the Creator's original and constant intention for his creatures in this world). Such a Resurrection, moreover, would offer in itself no promise of risen life beyond death for those who have to face both death and corruption. The miracle which we need would never yet have taken place.

In saying this I am not in any way denying the uniqueness and decisiveness of God's act in raising Jesus from the dead. Quite the contrary. I am not starting with a belief that all men are destined to survive death, and with a conviction that, because their bodies decay, this survival must somehow be in a non-material mode, and then arguing, from this belief, that if Jesus was truly man his Resurrection must therefore conform to the universal human pattern. The starting point must be the decisive event: Christ's Resurrection. It is unique, in the sense that, whereas we have no ground in ourselves for confidence that our destiny is to survive death, he was such that 'it was not possible for him to be held by it'. It was 'not possible' because of the perfection of his one-ness with the eternal and unchanging God. It is decisive because, through his unbroken union with the Father, his death and the overcoming of death in his Resurrection are, as Professor MacKinnon says, the act of God's final mercy, the victory which is the subduing of all things to the purposes of his mercy. Therefore, it is only in so far as we are, as Paul expresses it, 'in Christ', united with him by faith which responds to God's grace reaching out to us in him, that we may hope to be raised to a share in his risen life of communion with the eternal God.

Our hope is grounded in God's final affirmation of Jesus in raising him to life. This need not imply that the hope of certain pre-Christian Jews that those who died in faith and loyalty to God, especially those whose allegiance to him had led them to martyrdom, would be raised to life after death was vain. That hope was based, like our own, on confidence that God would not abandon, even in death, those whose lives had been centred upon him and who had responded faithfully to his call to serve him. Nor need we dismiss as empty illusion the hopes of men of other religions who have trusted in God, or the gods, to renew, after death, a relation of grace and communion with their servants. But for us Christ is the way, the truth and the life, and his Resurrection is the one pledge that our trust is not futile. And since our hope is to participate in his Resurrection life, and since we clearly cannot expect to be raised in our fleshly bodies, then our resurrection from death (which will not be physical) cannot be different in kind from his.

Professor MacKinnon's other most important contribution is his very proper contention that we must not consider the Resurrection of Christ in isolation, but in the closest relation to the nature and purpose of his Passion. He lays great emphasis on the decisiveness and uniqueness of both, as divine acts which are creative in themselves. He asks whether we are to regard the Cross as an *opus operatum* whose agent achieved something new, radically affected the scheme of things in time, and established in respect of the relations of men and women to God a new foundation: or whether we are compelled, partly by the demands of a theology that would emphasize divine acceptance above divine judgement, to say that all we find here is the most sublime presentation in time of the eternal readiness of God to receive to himself the truly penitent.

To the first part of the question my answer is unhesitatingly, Yes. In his death on the Cross Christ did achieve something new and established a new foundation for the relations of men and women to God. His death is a decisive act of God in history which changed the relation of man to himself for all time. It is decisive, because at this focal point in history men decisively rejected God in Christ, and God in Christ decisively accepted them by an act of sovereign love, which was at the same time his revelation of the measure of their sin and his judgement of it. It is *opus operatum*, an objective act, because its agent is not a good man setting the rest of mankind an example of noble conduct which may perhaps induce them to resolve to mend their ways, but is God Incarnate definitively declaring, as Professor Mac-Kinnon says in another context, his ways to man, in his once-for-all acceptance of man (at his very worst) with a sovereign love which judges man's sin, forgives the sinner, and transforms him by receiving him into communion with himself.

I prefer to avoid the term 'objective' in speaking of the Atonement, partly because of its obvious philosophical difficulties and partly because many theologians have assumed that the death of Christ can have objective efficacy only if it is an act directed either towards God, in satisfaction of his justice or in somehow making it possible for his love to operate for the forgiveness of sinners without compromising his holiness, or towards a personal devil in somehow liberating sinners from his clutches. I should wish, on the contrary, to say that the objective efficacy of the death of Christ lies in it being an act of God Incarnate directed towards man, placing him in a new relation to himself by a decisive act of acceptance.

For this reason I am unable to take the second part of Professor MacKinnon's question as contrary, or alternative, to the first. I should wish to say that the act of God in Christ on the Cross is both a decisive event in time which transformed man's relation to God, and also, since it certainly did not transform God's attitude to man, the most sublime presentation of that eternal attitude. It is indeed the focal point where that eternal attitude of love comes to a decisive and unique expression in the act of the Incarnate Son. But that act, by which the wholly impenitent are received (and judged in being received), set free and re-created, is not discontinuous with that eternal readiness to accept sinful men with invincible love, which was already revealed to such a prophet as Hosea. The God of Hosea was not an illusion. He is the God who acts in Christ, translating Hosea's vision into actuality and making it possible for men to repent, as Israel could not, because he assures them, in the most objective way possible, that they are already accepted by him.

I cannot set acceptance over against judgement as though there were any incompatibility between them. The Cross is a place of judgement and condemnation. Not of any judge-ment or condemnation of Jesus by God the Father. The judge is Jesus. Calvary is a place of execution, the execution of the Son of God by sinners, but by becoming this it is made to be Christ's judgement seat. Man's sin is disclosed there in its fullest odiousness. It is shown up and condemned by its encounter with steadfast love. Christ's acceptance of sinners is no easy tolerance. He offers no sanction for that artificial, blindly uncritical, 'Christian goodwill' which sometimes does duty for true charity. The Cross itself is the measure of the cost of acceptance. The width of the gulf between heaven and hell is revealed there, where the greatest act of human sin is wrought out in a darkness that covered all the land. Acceptance at the hands of the victim of that sin is itself the judgement and condemnation of sin; for it is only when the sinner is accepted that the judgement of his sin becomes effective, and only divine love is able to condemn sin by accepting the sinner. It makes no compro-mise with sin, nor does it need to be safeguarded from contamination by sinners, for it has sovereign power to reclaim them in the act of accepting them. Acceptance and judgement do not have to be balanced against each other. At the Cross the divine mercy, justice and truth are united, for they are inseparable aspects of that definitive declaration of the ways of God to man.

All this, which is only a part of what ought to be said about the Atonement, is not irrelevant to our discussion; for like Professor MacKinnon, though in a rather different way, I want to lay the greatest emphasis on the decisiveness and uniqueness of the Cross and the Resurrection In both these acts of God, however, I find no inconsistency between their decisiveness and 'objectivity' and the fact that they are directed towards men: the former as conveying to them the divine acceptance which is also judgement, the latter by bringing to them, in the Easter experiences, the active presence of the living Lord.

In something of the same way in which the story of the miraculous birth of Christ stands as a sign to indicate that in the life which the Gospels describe there is revealed a decisive act of God—that in that life we encounter one who is not mere man but God Incarnate—, so the story of the empty tomb stands as a sign to tell us that the transformation of the frightened and disillusioned disciples into apostles, and the emergence of the Christian community, are grounded in an objective act of God, of a decisive and final character. Read as factual history, however, it does nothing to guarantee the truth of the Christian conviction that God has raised Jesus from the dead: as witness the fact that from the legend of the guard in St Matthew's Gospel to the theory advanced recently by H. J. Schonfield, in *The Passover Plot*, the story of the empty tomb has persuaded many people, not that God acted in a unique and decisive way but that the body was stolen, that Jesus revived in the grave, and many other implausible hypotheses. Without the appearances, the empty tomb is not significant; and the reality of the presence of the living Lord, as it was known by his followers, needs no external confirmation by the empty tomb. Nothing, of course, but faith can in fact attest the truth of the Resurrection; and to look for some confirmation of its truth, independent of faith, would be, as both the present writers would agree, to 'seek after a sign' which 'shall not be given'.

8

FURTHER REFLECTIONS

D. M. MacKinnon

Professor MacKinnon adds some further thoughts on Professor Lampe's position, and concludes the dialogue by briefly indicating the philosophical pre-suppositions which affect his own thinking on these issues.

8

FURTHER REFLECTIONS

D. M. MacKinnon

I SHOULD like to begin by expressing my gratitude for Professor Lampe's very valuable and searching comments on what I have written. In what follows I will not attempt to answer his arguments in detail, still less to score points against him; the matters we are concerned with are too difficult and too crucial to admit of such treatment; I shall therefore merely try to indicate where and why I still venture to differ from him.

I welcome very much the reference he makes, towards the end of what he has written, to the significance of the book of Hosea. This section of his argument, and indeed the whole burden of his comment, seem to show clearly that what in the end is raised by the issues we have been discussing, is the relation of the temporal to the eternal. This is, of course, a metaphysical problem; but it is a metaphysical problem that is transformed in Christian theology by the doctrine of the Incarnation. In one of the most illuminating remarks I have ever encountered on the relations of philosophy and theology, the late Professor A. N. Whitehead spoke of Christianity as a religion perennially in search of a metaphysic, but never able to rest in one. While this is a remark which has many different applications, one of its senses bears on the issues that divide Professor Lampe and myself; the issues on which I touched when I suggested in my earlier comments on our material that we needed to thrash out the significance of the notion of *dependence* in its theological employment. Is there a sense in which *sub specie aeternitatis* Hosea's acceptance of Gomer *depends* upon the work of God in Christ? If I understand him aright, it is one of Karl Barth's profoundest insights that there is: I say 'insights' and I pause, recalling how Dr Olive Wyon (a most experienced translator of German theology) remarked to me once in conversation that where Barth is concerned, for all the massiveness and intellectual power of his argument, one is in the end dealing with a poet rather than an exegete.

Certainly, if I turn again to that parable which, perhaps before all others, speaks of acceptance, namely the parable of the two brothers, there is one point which I am bound to repeat. Whatever the context in which this parable was first spoken, whatever general thesis we may hold of the function of parable in Christ's teaching, we are given here a story which, in fact, describes a raw piece of human life. Emphatically, to use a modern classification, it does not belong to the genre of 'light romance'! The relation of the father to the two brothers in the climax of the tale is an analogy of the ways of God with men. But to treat that father *in himself* as a portrayal of the Divine is surely to be guilty of sheer anthropomorphism. We can see in him, in his all too human ambivalence, the makings (as I said) on a different occasion of a Lear who falls ready victim to the blandishments of a Goneril and a Regan, and rejects the truth spoken by a Cordelia. We have to reckon with the *precariousness* of human goodness; I say to reckon with it, neither plunged by its recognition into despair, nor evading its acknowledgement in order to defend against all criticism that goodness whose reality we feel menaced, if once we admit the threats that hang over it.

What I want to suggest is that we have to see the work of God in Christ as that which secures against the ever-present menace of their dissolution, our frail, but genuine, human perceptions and affirmations (in action) of the morally excellent. It is a curious fact that while the general culture of contemporary theologians is still markedly literary, rather than scientific, they seem to forget the many lessons concerning the human situation to be learnt from tragedy, whether ancient or modern. Thus, to take one example: recently I re-read the *Electra* of Sophocles, and was amazed by the depth with which it uncovered the degradation into a creature consumed by, indeed virtually living by, the hatred which possesses her, of a woman who initially had simply refused to compromise with truth, and to pretend the situation at the court of Aegisthus and Clytemnestra to be other than itself. Certainly, in the play she is presented also as a woman afraid for her life, as well as desolated by the grief of Orestes' supposed death. But it is part of the dramatist's mastery of his theme that he makes her compromising, accommodating sister Chrysothemis a more attractive and sympathetic figure. Yet what has betrayed Electra but her fidelity to truth and justice? And something of the same sort applies in the case of Deianira in the *Trachiniae*; it is her tenderness towards her formidable husband, and her compassion for Iole, which tempt her into ultimately destructive folly. Something of the same sort may surely be said of Brutus, as Shakespeare portrays him in *Julius Caesar*, especially if his scrupulous self-interrogation is contrasted with the quick, murderous resolution of the proscribing triumvirs. If we say that in the crucifixion and Resurrection of Christ we have advanced 'beyond tragedy', we need, in order to understand what we are saying, to take stock of what tragedy is. Maybe we need (this is very tentative) to alert ourselves more than we do to the tragic elements lying just beneath the surface of the parabolic, and even to receive what is offered to us as tragedy as parable, at least in an extended use of that already comprehensive concept.[1]

It is with such considerations as these in mind that I would wish to speak of the act of God in Christ as objective, as something built into the structure of the world, even perhaps (as I think that Barth would argue) its very foundation. Indeed, I remember that Barth enthusiastically welcomed a remark of the late Dorothy Sayers, in her broadcast plays, that we are dealing here with 'the only thing that ever really happened'. Although Barth rejected the *analogia entis*, he has had his own doctrine of degrees of event-hood!

There are, in the history of philosophy, continually renewed controversies between those who, where the theory of knowledge is concerned, are commonly called realists, and those who are sometimes called idealists, but also constructivists, between those for whom truth resides in the end in correspondence between proposition and fact, and those for whom it is something brought into being by more or less autonomous understanding. It is, of course, a mark of the very greatest philosophers, of Kant for instance, that they have sought the middle way between those two positions, or rather have sought to do justice to the insights both contained. In contemporary philosophy of science, what gives its commanding significance to the work deriving from Sir Karl Popper's book, *The Logic of Scientific Investigation* (Hutchinson, 1958), is an analogous attempt to fuse, in an exact account of theoretical activity in the sciences, the moments of creativity and of finding. Yet one cannot in the end escape some sort of choice concerning the place where one acknowledges the last word spoken on questions of truth and falsity: is it that which is found to be the case, or

[1] Again I would refer to the extended treatment of the relation of the parabolic to the tragic in the second series of my Gifford lectures. There the whole discussion is connected with the question of the relation of the familiar to the transcendent on which it depends and to which it bears witness.

is it that which satisfies the demand of the self-regulating intellect? I suspect that, very much as Coleridge said that all men were at bottom either Platonists or Aristotelians, so we are, most of us, if we are informed enough philosophically to be self-conscious about these things, idealists or realists. Moreover, I further suspect that one's state of mind on these matters is reflected in one's theological attitudes, and that for good or for ill. In the end I know that my own bias is always in the realists' direction, and that therefore I am (perhaps quite unfairly) hostile to views which seem to me to *move* in the direction of saying that faith creates its own objectives. I say *move* in this direction: for it is manifestly utterly unfair to Professor Lampe's position to suggest that he does anything of the sort. Yet I must admit that my readiness to use objectivist language more freely than he does may have its roots (at least in part) in an eagerness, in questions of general epistemology, to endorse the views of those who emphasize the element of *discovery* in coming to know, and the authority of brute *fact* in the refutation of hypotheses.

It is perhaps valuable to seem to digress in this way, if only to bring out into the open conflicts of attitude that may be reflected in one's theological judgement, although their roots lie in quite general considerations of another sort. Thus, I realize that I almost certainly tend to over-emphasize the extent to which faith must be construed as following after, or corresponding with, something antecedently given, and to under-emphasize the extent to which it is a constituent moment in a whole purpose that is, in the last resort, incomplete without it. I have to reckon with the degree to which my theological thought may be vitiated by a readiness to conceive or to represent the work of atonement in ways that depreciate the extent to which it necessarily includes within it personal response on the part of those who are (to use traditional language) recipients of its benefits. Against this I can plead that while my philosophical *parti pris* may betray me into distortion in this respect, it also enables me to do justice to something clearly glimpsed by Dix in the passage from *The Shape of the Liturgy*, to which I referred in my comments, as well as by Barth and by P. T. Forsyth.

Clearly, these last considerations are also relevant to the difference there is between Professor Lampe and myself, where the tradition of the empty tomb is concerned. It is because I seek after *facts* (rather than after 'a sign' in the sense of the sort of evident manifestation which I agree with him it would be radically wrong to seek) that I look for a publicly observable state of affairs in the spatial and temporal world, not disclosing, nor containing, but still pointing towards (in a way that I agree remains entirely ambivalent) that which is, in my view, necessarily *unique* and creative. What discussion I have had with him of these issues has enabled me to see more clearly (apart altogether from the numerous points of detail on which his scholarship and insight have illuminated my understanding) the extent to which here a whole number of different questions are knotted together. Thus I conclude, at the risk of repetition, these last remarks by saying that what I now find I want most to do is to clarify a little, if I can, the notion of *dependence* as we employ it in these contexts. It is not without significance to notice that it is a notion whose exploration plunges one at once into the ethical intimacies of soteriology, and the abstract styles of the philosophy of logic. Advance in theological understanding demands, in a measure, a combination of both manners of reflection!